With Him in Glory

LARRY CLIFTON

ISBN 979-8-89130-878-7 (paperback)
ISBN 979-8-89130-879-4 (digital)

Copyright © 2024 by Larry Clifton

All rights reserved. No part of this publication may be reproduced, distributed, or transmitted in any form or by any means, including photocopying, recording, or other electronic or mechanical methods without the prior written permission of the publisher. For permission requests, solicit the publisher via the address below.

Christian Faith Publishing
832 Park Avenue
Meadville, PA 16335
www.christianfaithpublishing.com

Printed in the United States of America

```
                    J
                    E
                    S
                    U
                    S
YOU ARE MY LORD SAVIOR AND REDEEMER
                    H
                    A
                    V
                    E
                    M
                    E
                    R
                    C
                    Y
                    O
                    N
                    U
                    S
                    S
                    I
                    N
                    N
                    E
                    R
                    S
```

Finding Jesus

```
E U S I J J S S E E U E J
J E S U S E E J U U U E
S S S S U U E U J J J S S
U U U U S S E S J E J U
S E S E S J U J S S S S S
J U U S S E E J J J J J J
E E S S U U J J S E E E J
S S S S S S S U U U U U
U U U U U U S S S S S S
E E S S J J U U S E J U U
```

If you successfully found Jesus, pray to him. Confess that He is the Savior, the Son of God. Believe that He rose from the dead and is alive today in this world.

Losing Hope

Hurt, fear, confusion, and the feeling of betrayal all lead to the victim having a poor self-image of himself or herself, which accompanies victimization. Something is wrong inside. Many victims may see themselves as being weak or naive. That is because we allow Satan to set up camp in our hearts and minds. We allow him (Satan) to crush what faith we had built up in the name of Jesus.

When the spirit of a victim has been crushed, this person sometimes falls into a depressive state that results in downheartedness, self-pity, shame, resentment, and hate for fellow men and women, which we all know leads to sin, for hate is the highest form of sin. When you hate your fellow man or woman, the Father frowns on that because His Word says to love your neighbor as yourself. Living in love erases the hate you feel for others; love removes despair; love destroys anger. If you live and walk in the spirit of our Lord and Savior, you walk in love for each person with whom you come in contact. The spirit of the Savior is *love*.

> For creation was condemned to lose its purpose, not of its own will, but because God willed it to be so. Yet there was the hope that creation itself would one day be set free from its slavery to decay and would share the glorious freedom of the children of God. (Romans 8:20–21)

Self-doubt invites despair and hopelessness. When hope is no longer there, what is left? It doesn't always have to be like that. For when you are a child of the Father, there is always hope. He made sure of that by sending His only begotten Son, Jesus Christ, to be our redeemer and wash away all doubt from our minds.

Don't be a doubting Thomas!

> Do not fear those who kill the body but cannot kill the soul. But rather fear Him who is able to destroy both soul and body in hell. (Matthew 10:28)

The enemy of the soul (Satan) has us believe we are not important enough to the Father. He wants us to be down on ourselves in such a way as to manipulate us into thinking that we have no value to the Father. But if that were true, why did He (the Father) send His one and only Son to be the sacrificial Lamb to be sacrificed for our sins if we had no value to the Father?

From before the creation of the world, our Heavenly Father had made plans for each and every person's life. Where you find the truth about the Father and ourselves is through knowing and listening to the spirit of Jesus Christ who dwells in our hearts.

> For in Him dwells all the fullness of the Godhead bodily; and you are complete in Him who is the head of all principality and power. In Him you were also circumcised with the circumcision made without hands, by putting off the body of the sin of the flesh, but the circumcision of Christ. (Colossians 2:9–11)

Hopelessness is just a way that Satan tricks you in his devious act of putting doubt in your walk with the Father. Hopelessness cannot enslave us when we see ourselves as the Father sees us—*full of the Holy Spirit*! In conclusion, my brothers and sisters, do not be so down on yourselves. Don't let Satan rain on your parade as you walk with the Father!

Let us pray: Heavenly Father, open the eyes of Your believers to see themselves as You see them. Thank You, Father. In Jesus's name, amen!

Many abused victims, by harming themselves, don't have normal thoughts. To them, the pain and loss of self-worth are more than they desire to handle. It is so great that many find no alternative other than self-destruction. Judas is a prime example of allowing Satan to use him.

He was one of Jesus's apostles when he allowed Satan to use him to betray Jesus. He had witnessed many miracles Jesus had performed. Yet because of greed, he betrayed Jesus for thirty pieces of silver. After this act of betrayal, he felt remorse and a loss of hope; he went out and committed suicide.

> Then he (Judas) threw down the pieces of silver in the temple and departed, and went and hanged himself. (Matthew 27:5)

Clearly, this was not the work of the Father. It was the work of Satan, wouldn't you say? He (Satan) will try to steal your hope and faith in the Father by trying to convince his victims that his alternative of death is best.

But that is just one of the many lies he wants you to believe. No matter how hopeless our lives may seem, the Father gives hope to those who believe.

> May God, the source of hope, fill you all with joy and peace by means of your faith in Him, so that your hope will continue to grow by the power of the Holy Spirit. (Romans 15:13)

Let us pray: Father in heaven, give me hope and all joy so that others may see and come to know You. O Lord, strengthen my faith and love for You so that I can pass it on to others. In the name of Jesus, amen!

Christmas Time

Christmas is the time of year for the Lord on high to be praised and worshipped throughout the world. For He was born to the world to try and change the way things were and to give hope to those who had none. It is the time of the year to be giving thanks to the Father on high. It's the time to be thankful and caring toward everyone we meet, especially family.

The time to praise the newborn King. Let the bells ring out joy and love to all the world. Let us sing and rejoice in His holy and glorious name. Being thankful that He came to earth to set the world free from all sin, even though He was nailed to a tree, to give everlasting life and salvation to *you* and to me!

I praise You, Lord Father, for making me, a lowly sinner, see all the wonders of Thee. Christmas time is the greatest time of year for those who have ears to hear, and for those who know the true meaning of the season. Talk to the Lord, and He will fill you with Christmas cheer and make it clear that Christmas is a special time without any fear.

Give the Lord some Christmas cheer that all the angels can hear. There is no unhappiness because the Lord holds you dear to His spirit. He can provide you with a new start. From Him, you will never part. So hold on tight to the Savior dear. Let the world know of the newborn King. He is here! Keep the King in your heart so that Christmas reigns *all* year long!

Merry Christmas!

Jesus Walks with Me

Jesus walks with me
Everywhere I go
He is the One that saved
My wretched soul
When I had nowhere to go
But the fiery pits of damnation
Jesus walks with me.
In the dark and the light
He will walk with you too.
Just reach out and take His hand,
Say no to worldly passions.
Jesus doesn't just forgive our sins
He frees us from destructive lifestyles.
He renews your faith in self
When you turn left,
He turns you right.
When anyone cries out to Him for help,
He's with us,
Offering hope for the future.
With that *salvation*!
Jesus walks with me!

Why You Were Made

You, my brethren, were made in the image of the Father. What does it mean to be made in the image of the Father? When He created you, He gave you a heart to love and feelings for other people. For those who seek after the Father, He gives the same power that His Son has, making you heirs to the kingdom. So, my brethren, when you become a born-again child of the Father filled with the Holy Spirit of the Lord and Savior, you become a full-fledged citizen of the *kingdom on high*.

When the Father made you, He had a special reason in mind. By being born into sin, you already have one point against you. Sin is the nature of the human race; we are separated from the Father.

He had to make a way for those who seek after the graces of the Creator. He sent His only Son to be the payment for the world's sins. By grace, you are saved and only by grace. There is no amount of good that you can do to get saved. For those who have the grace of the Father and are called by Him, their purpose is to spread the good news of how to gain salvation and everlasting life. Just because you are saved doesn't mean that you have the ability to save souls; it only means that you are able to talk to people about how the Father has changed your life.

The Father is the only one who has the power to save souls. Because the Father is *grace* and freely gives grace to those He has called, people have to make up their own minds as to whether they want the Savior in their lives, or do they want to remain in the state that they are now living—*in the flesh without the spirit of the Lord and Savior Jesus Christ*. That is their decision to make, not yours. Yours is to show them your deep love for our Savior. Not only is it for *you* to get to know Him (Jesus), but also to praise His holy name and do His will to make the world a better place to live.

You can't and won't be truly satisfied until you know the Father personally. The Bible tells us how we can personally get to know His wondrous love, grace, peace, and kindness. The answer we need to know must come from outside this world. No matter which road you take, when you know the Lord Jesus, He will take the wheel and steer you in the right direction, which is the narrow road to the *Father on high*.

Heavenly Father, I understand why You made me, and I realize that I am truly a child of the Father. In Jesus's name, thank You!

The God Who Redeems

When I was out in the world doing all kinds of unholy acts of disobedience and rebellious things against the Father, He never gave up on me. He restored what was broken with His redeeming love and grace. The Father I now serve is a faithful, loving, caring, and forgiving Father. Even when we are unfaithful to Him, He is always faithful and forgiving toward us who don't deserve His everlasting love and understanding. Like myself, who had made such a mess out of my life, the Father, by His love and grace, put His arms around me and pulled me back to where I belong—*in His loving care*. So don't ever in your mind think you are unworthy of the Father's love and care.

He loves you so much that He sent His Son, Jesus Christ, to take all the sins of this world upon His shoulders and die for us so that we didn't have to. The wages of sin is death, which Jesus Christ had already borne for us. Those who come to the Father and repent of their sins and ask forgiveness need not worry, for our faithful Father will open His arms, forgive us, and give us everlasting life to live in heaven with Him and our Savior, who loves us just as much.

In Isaiah 42:18–19, the prophet Isaiah rebuked the people of Israel for their spiritual blindness and deafness.

> Hear, you deaf, and look, you blind, that you may see. Who is blind but my servant, or deaf as my messenger whom I send? Who is blind as he who is perfect, and blind as the Lord's servant?

Bring all your cares and worries to the God who redeems!

Sick and Tired

If you are sick and tired
Of being sick and tired

Lay down all your pride
Place it on the side
Come to the light, and don't hide
For in the Lord, you must confide
For in the devil, there is no free ride
The Lord too long you have denied
In the name of the Lord, you must abide
Tell that devil that he has lied

Christ's death on that tree
Set the whole world free

No longer do we need to be sick and tired
Now to a new life we have aspired

Sustainer of Blessings

> Remember the Lord your God, for it is He who gives you the ability to produce wealth and so confirms His covenant, which He swore to your ancestors as it is today. (Deuteronomy 8:18)

Sometimes, even good things can overwhelm us unexpectedly. We, as humans, have the tendency to take matters into our own hands. Then when everything turns into too much for us to handle, we turn to the Father for help, which is the wrong approach.

We seem to forget about the One who gave us the ability to do the things we do. We want to take all the credit for ourselves and leave God out. If it had not been for the Lord Jesus, we would not be able to do the things we do. Give the Father His just credit. My brethren, everything you do is because of the grace of the Father, who gives us our strength. For we are weak in the flesh. Without the help and power of our Lord and Savior Jesus Christ, King of kings and Lord of lords, all-powerful and loving, we would not be able to enjoy all good things, including physical health and the skills needed to earn a living. All come from the blessings of the Father, *for He surely is the sustainer of our blessings!*

Stewardship and Giving

Joy is a by-product of God-nudged giving. The Father loves a cheerful giver. When you give from the heart, not reluctantly or under compulsion, each of you should give what you have decided in your heart to give. Paul instructed the Corinthians in the art of generosity—*to give from the heart*. Remember this: Those who sow sparingly will reap sparingly, but those who sow generously will reap generously.

Dear One

Know that the Father is here
Sweet one, nothing to fear

The Lord is by your side
Tell the devil to run and hide
No more listen to how he has lied

'Cause, dear one, the Father sees you
Don't be so blue
For all the hard times you went through
He knows so well; He went through them too

Let Him ease your pain
So you won't become insane

Live your life by His Word
Yes, it was your cries He heard.

Dear one, put your trust in the Father!

Jesus Lives Forever

God's plan of salvation, along with Jesus's death and resurrection, began a new era in the lives of the people of the world. For time and eternity, what His resurrection accomplished was of great significance. It seemed that when Jesus died, the evil of the world was in control. Yet by Sunday morning, three days later, a far-superior power had taken over. The Father had acted to show the world that He was yet in control of the event all the time. Something had changed; now the world had a Savior.

The Father acted with a power that overcame the Roman guards, and the stone was rolled away. A great earthquake occurred. From the grip of death, Jesus was set free to overcome death forever. By raising His Son from death, the Father gave great honor.

> The God of Abraham, Isaac, and Jacob, the God of our Fathers, glorified His Servant Jesus, whom you denied in the presence of Pilate, when he was determined to let him go. But you denied the Holy One and the Just, and asked for a murderer to be granted to you, and killed the Prince of life, whom God raised from the dead, of which we are witnesses. (Acts 3:13–15)

> Let it be known to you all, and to all the people of Israel, that by the name of Jesus Christ of Nazareth, whom you crucified, whom God raised from the dead, by Him this man stands here before you whole. (Acts 4:10–11)

Over all demonic power, the resurrection placed Christ in a position of authority.

> Which He wrought in Christ when He raised Him from the dead, and set Him at His own right hand in the heavenly places, far above all principality and power and might and dominion, and every name that is named, not only in this world, but also in that which is to come. (Ephesians 1:20–21)

Give your life to Jesus and live forever!

May Your Kingdom Come

Father, let Your kingdom come; Your will be done
Keep that devil on the run
Satan shall not have any fun
Thank you, Father, for Your Son
Knowing You makes my heart shine like the *sun*,

Father, let my light shine
To keep me in line
To me, Father, You are one of a kind
Open my eyes to what I am—*blind*.
For it is You, Lord, I seek to find.

I know it is not for me to ask why
But to serve You until I die
With belief in Satan, you will live a lie

In the middle of my war, it was You, Lord, that took control.
Lord Father, lead me back to Your fold

Satan: a Defeated Foe

The Lord Jesus stated in His preaching about the church that the gates of hell would not prevail against it. As members of the body of Christ, we will ultimately be victorious in our fight against Satan. Through His death and resurrection, Christ won the war with Satan. Thus, we are fighting a foe that has already been defeated. We can find throughout the Bible God's promise of victory over Satan and his army.

A good illustration is the cat and the dog of how the follower of Jesus should react toward Satan. When a cat is faced with a dog, normally if there is some place safe for him (the cat), like a tree, he will run up that tree. But if there is no place safe, the cat will arch its back and spit at the dog. The average dog will turn and run off from the fighting cat. We, too, must be like the cat and call Satan's bluff. When we have the armor of the Father and face Satan squarely and resist his advance, he, too, will turn tail and run.

> So place yourselves under God's authority. Resist the devil and will run away from you. (James 4:7)

Satan was defeated by Christ at the cross; that in itself is the basis of our victory over Satan. Jesus judged the devil and overthrew him. This world is being judged now.

> Now is the time for judgment on the world; now the prince of this world will be driven out, and I, when I am lifted up from the earth, will draw all people to myself. (John 12:31–32 and 16:11)

Be strong in the Father for Satan is already a defeated foe!

Finish Strong in Your Spiritual Diet

The Word of the Father (the Bible) compares physical life with spiritual life. The Father created humankind to worship Him, not worship the world like so many of us do. To prosper and grow, both physical and spiritual must be properly nourished and nurtured. Here we have Paul placing himself in the hands of the Lord. This same Paul, formerly named Saul, was a persecutor of all the Christian people. Paul's family was of the tribe of Benjamin. He was educated in Jerusalem in the Jewish religion according to the tradition of his ancestors.

Becoming a true believer in Christ is a matter of birth (the new birth), a matter of growth in the knowledge of our Lord and Savior Jesus Christ. Believers are urged to grow in the grace of our Lord. For proper growth and development in humankind, we must nourish ourselves with various foods—*physical foods*. By receiving the graces bestowed upon believers by our Lord, we receive a different type of food—*spiritual food*. Through the feeding and care of the Father, we have been richly provided for to grow and develop our *spiritual* life. For the soul, His Word, the Holy Bible, contains a diet providing every spiritual vitamin needed for health and growth.

Thank You, Heavenly Father, for Your spiritual diet so that I can finish strong! In Your name!

Enjoy Life

We should enjoy life
While being able
The Father will be coming back
To redeem His people
There are some
Who will not be ready
When it's time to go home
Place all your affairs
In order
Then be ready
Be happy with the life you have
Which the Father gave you
For a very special reason
Love
He gave you the family you have
To share His *love* with each other
So much to be thankful for
Family is a gift
From the all-powerful and caring *Father*!
For there are many living without hope or love
Stop to realize how fortunate *you* are
To have what you've been given
Someone who truly *loves* you
No matter what
Give all the praise to the Father
If not for His love
Many would have no love at all
Enjoy life in the Savior
Be thankful for our gracious God!

Cleanse Me

Cleanse me, merciful Father
Have mercy on me
For I have sinned
Greatly against You
Cleanse me, O Lord,
In Your redeeming blood
Wash all my sins away
Make me white
As the first driven snow
Restore to me the gladness
Of Your salvation
Grant me, O Lord,
The Holy Spirit
To guide my heart
In Your loving ways
Of all my iniquities, O Lord,
I repent
Take them from me
Throw them into the sea of forgiveness
To nevermore remember
Renew in me a steadfast spirit
Place in me, Lord Father,
A willing heart
Cleanse me, Father
In the blood of the Lamb!

To the Lord

Lord Father,
You are the bright morning star
Shining so bright from afar
To me, Father,
That is who You really are

You lead me
All through the dark night
Lord Father,
I pray You keep me in Your sight
Bring me, Father, from the dark
Back into the light

Come, all that thirst
Let the heavenly Father
Put you first
Fill me with joy, Father,
Until I burst

All the blessings in my life
You will stack
Nevermore will I turn my back
Lord Father, You can count on that!

In Evil Long

In evil long there I stood, just like a sinner from the hood. I was unmoved by shame and fear, not really wanting to hear that tiny little voice in my ear. It wasn't until a new object struck my sight that I saw the light, which stopped my wild career!

In a dream, I saw someone hanging from a tree, just wanting to save you and me in His agony, so we and the world can be *free*! Below this cross, I stood, thinking about all He must have gone through, while all the time being so holy and true. He fixed His bloodstained eyes on me, where He could see how much this really hurt me. As I near the cross, I stood with tears in my eyes, just wishing that He should not have had to go through it, I felt so defeated and heartbroken!

It seemed to charge my sin, my weak flesh. I fell down on my knees, destined to confess. Never will I forget that look, for when I cried, my shoulders shook. All I could do was cry out, "Lord, please put my name in Your book!"

It charged me with His death, though not a word He spoke. My conscience felt and owned the guilt, wrapping around me like a quilt and plunging me into despair.

Please tell me, how can this be fair? I saw my sins His precious blood had spilled. I believe He washed away all my guilt and all my sins which helped to nail Him there. *My Lord Jesus really did care, my savior and redeemer!*

Love That Forgives

There is a love that forgives, which only comes from the Holy Spirit of the one and only Person that gave His life so that we can be free to receive that love: *Our Lord and Savior Jesus Christ!*

To help believers in Jesus, there is a scripture written to help us live together in unity. Paul refers to the essential role forgiveness plays,

> Therefore, as the elect of God, holy and beloved, put on tender mercies, kindness, humility, meekness, longsuffering, bearing with one another, if anyone has a complaint against another, even as Christ forgave you, so you also must do. But above all these things put on love, which is the bond of perfection. (Colossians 3:12–14)

All interactions with each other are to be guided with love and understanding, most importantly. Outlined by Paul are the characteristics and blessings found in relationships modeled upon forgiveness and love for one another. When you believe in the Father, He will help all of us who believe in cultivating these healthy relationships. *Love to forgive!*

God's Promise

God's promise of redemption is always certain because He cannot lie. The Father's works we can't always understand. Sometimes we even wonder if He is working at all. We know that God always remembers His promise because He is God, the Creator of all things and people. The Word of the Father is like depositing money in your bank account; it's always there—no worries about using it up.

His promise is at work, guiding our footsteps each day to keep us on the up and up. Therefore, there can be no mistake as to how the believers in Christ should conduct themselves for the glory of the Father. Perhaps you aren't sure His promise of redemption is always certain. To overcome this disbelief, one uses prayer.

Prayer is simply calling upon God. When we call on the Lord, He is faithful and caring when our prayers reach Him. He doesn't turn anyone's prayers away. In His time, your prayers will be answered. Just remember, one day we will fully experience His presence in the glory of heaven, as Jesus is our intercessor to the Father's right hand. You can have full confidence the Father hears your prayers through our Lord and Savior Jesus Christ. It matters not whether your prayers are short or imperfect in your eyes. *Jesus is our go-between to the Father. His love for you is eternal according to his promise. Live your life on the promise of the Father!*

Forgiving Others

When we forgive people who have hurt us in one way or the other, it takes a huge load off our shoulders. Not only does it lighten our burden we have been carrying around all this time, it allows for peace of mind. This also reminds us of our humanness for which we are always at war. So often, we hold on too tightly to the things we should release, such as unforgiveness or fault. An unforgiving heart eventually leads to unhealthy feelings toward other people.

Let go and let God! Give your unforgiving heart over to the Father and place your trust in Him instead of holding on to what we as humans have no control over. You are giving it all over to the One who has the power to overcome such things. Satan is right there, feeding off our downfalls. He knows how to latch on and cause all manner of hurt.

For the Father is sheer mercy and grace and not easily angered but rich in love. He doesn't always remind us of our faults, which every one of us has. He never holds grudges as we often do. In fact, the Father doesn't see us in the same light as everyone else. He only sees the good in people, the same way we should also see. But it doesn't work out that way since we as humans live in the *flesh*. The flesh can be a mighty ruler in our lives when we allow it to be so. Forgiveness shown to others allows us to become *free*. Let God do His power and might. So, my brethren, turn all your hurts and wounds placed by others upon ourselves to the Father and defeat the *flesh*! Hold not onto anger which builds up resentments and eventually spreads enmity between people. Our Father loves us! Release your hurts, angers, and resentments to Him, and let Him work His magic!

Walk as Jesus

We need to follow in Jesus's footsteps if we call ourselves disciples of the Lord. As John said, we need to live in the way that Jesus did while here on earth.

> Those who say they live in God should live
> their lives as Jesus did. (1 John 2:6)

We, as believers in the Father, should live our lives and walk in a way that shows in our behavior toward others that there is no doubt as to our love for the Father. When you say you are a child of the Father, that should be obvious in the way you walk and talk.

When other people look at you, they should be able to see the workings of the Holy Spirit in your actions, the same as people saw in Jesus Christ. If we can't shine like Jesus, we need to look deep inside ourselves and ask the Lord to reveal what it is that we need to change to shine. Make time in your life for the Father each and every day. Hang on to His Word. Spend time with Him in fellowship throughout the day.

To disciples who stay close to Christ, there is a tremendous benefit. The Father wants us to be imitators of Him. When you look up to someone you really love, you try to imitate that person. So it is with the Father; live your life with love in your eyes, and in the end, you will turn your life around and walk like Jesus.

Father, Help Me

Help me, Lord Father, to place all my trust and faith in You.
Lord Father, You are what my heart thirsts for.
Father God, I thank You for Your astounding
love gift—life in Jesus Christ.
Father, Your love overwhelms me.
Thank You, Lord, for the promise that You will meet all my needs.
Help me not to fear or doubt.
I am grateful that You are watching over me.
My cries for help reach Your perfect ears.
Loving Father, I long to follow You completely
Always in times of drought or times of abundance.
Help me to turn to You in my hour of dire need.
Thank You, Father, for affirming that I
don't need to know everything.
What lies ahead is not important.
I know that You, Father, never change.
Lord, thank You for Your Word—*the Bible*.
Your Word provides me with wisdom,
understanding, and hope for the future.
Please help me, Father, to be more humble to people.
Please help me to listen to You and trust You are in control.
Teach me, Heavenly Father, to be more thankful.
Help me to see You for who You really are
Not who Satan tries to make You out to be.
You provide joy that is beyond anything that
devious Satan can ever offer me.
Help me show and share Your joy with others wherever I go.
I will glorify Your holy name forever.

Satan's Kingdom

As Christians, we are daily faced with decisions that have a great impact on us. In this world, we find so much that can cause us to separate from our Lord and Savior. The demons of Satan are alive and well in humanity. In the kingdom of Satan, there are numerous demons that belong to the prince of darkness and act under his direction. We are surrounded by the darkness of the evil spirits that prowl around the world in search of souls.

They try to discourage, distress, perplex, and harass those who are seeking to honor Christ. Since they (demons) cannot get to the Lord Jesus Christ, they turn their attention to the Lord's representatives—*Christians*, who are part of the body of Christ. Therefore, satanic forces seek to destroy the body by opposing its service and spiritual growth. To recognize Satan's work, we just need to take a look at what is happening in the world today. Crime, acts of violence, immoral living, etc., all contribute to the power that Satan has over humanity. We as Christians need to be on our guard and stay strong in the Father and continue to fight the forces who are trying to destroy us.

According to Ephesians 6, Satan's kingdom is comprised of four divisions: principalities, powers, rulers of the darkness, and wicked spirits in heavenly places. In verse 12, we read,

> For we wrestle not against flesh and blood, but against principalities, against powers, against the rulers of darkness of this world, and against spiritual wickedness in high places.

Demon forces and fallen angels are under him. In the Bible, we read in various places that Satan has divided this world into sections or provinces, each controlled by a prince (demon).

Heavenly Father, keep us safe from the evil powers of the kingdom of Satan and his demon spirits!

Morning Offering

My God, heavenly Father, I adore You
That is why I live my life
Only for You, Lord
Father, I love You with all my heart
Each day I pray for a new start
One that will never drive us apart
Lord Father, shine Your light upon me
So I do not lose my way
As I walk in Your sight
I come to honor You, Holy Father
Day and night
Father, may Your grace always be with me
Until I see Your sweet face
Lord Father, You keep me in my place
While I run life's glorious race.

Call on the Father and seek your morning offering!

Jesus Is Coming in Justice

Lord Father, give me a hunger for Your justice. Help me be a healing part of Your work in doing what is right. Jesus said,

> Blessed are those who hunger and thirst for righteousness, for they will be filled. (Matthew 5:6)

One day, Jesus will be coming back to claim His people, deliver justice, and right the wrongs. But until that time approaches, we have the opportunity to serve a gracious, loving, caring, and forgiving Father. We will participate in the Father's justice in reality on earth just as He promised over two thousand years before His death.

In Isaiah 58, he paints a vivid picture of what the Father calls His people to do. Here are a few of those requests from the Father—do not turn away from those who need help, clothe the naked, provide the poor wanderers with shelter, and loose the chains of injustice. One way our lives point back to the Father is by seeking justice for the oppressed and the marginalized.

Isaiah writes that His people seeking justice is like the light of dawn and results in healing for them as well as for others.

> Then your light shall break forth like the morning star, and your righteousness shall go before you; the glory of the Lord shall be your rear guard. (Isaiah 58:8)

Today, here on Earth, may the Father help us to cultivate a hunger for His righteousness. The Bible says as we seek justice in His way and in His power, we'll be satisfied in His righteousness. *Seek the father before his return*!

To Reveal the Father

Jesus came to earth not only to save the lost but also to reveal the Father to the world as well as to bring hope to the poor and salvation to those who wholeheartedly seek everlasting life. We read this truth in John 1:18 where it says,

> "No one has ever seen God, but the one and only Son, who is himself God and is in closest relationship with the Father, has made Him known. Those who have Him (Jesus) have seen the Father," Jesus declared.

Hebrews 1:3 tells us that Christ is the image of the person of the Father. The Father is invisible and also a great spirit. No one is able to see Him with the physical eye. At some point, we all have asked the question, "What is God like?"

To look at Jesus is one way we can know something about the nature of the Father. Jesus came so that we, as limited humans, might see the Father and so that we might better know what He is like. For Apostle Paul said,

> For it is the Father who said, let light shine out of darkness, make His light shine in our hearts to give us the light of the knowledge of God's glory displayed in the face of Christ. (2 Corinthians 4:6)

The apostle John says,

> The Word was made flesh, and dwelt among us. (John 1:14)

In Israel, generation after generation of people looked for the Messiah. Soon after Adam and Eve were driven out of the Garden of Eden, they looked for the promised Redeemer. But one night, nearly two thousand years ago, the Father stepped out of the frame of the universe and appeared on earth in the person of our Lord and Savior, King of kings, Jesus Christ in the flesh. Jesus came to this earth so that we might learn to know better what the Father is like.

Lord Jesus, thank You for coming to this sinful earth not only to redeem the lost but to reveal the Father so we may get to know Him better. In Jesus's name, amen!

About Anger

What does the Bible say about anger?

> Let go of anger and abandon rage; do not become upset and turn to doing evil. For evil men and women will be done away with, but those hoping in the Father will possess the earth. (Psalm 37:8–9)

Handling anger is a delicate and important topic. Christian counselors report that many clients seeking help come to counseling and have problems dealing with anger issues either by being pushed into anger or by some other means.

Anger ruins both the joy and health of many. It can shatter communication and tear apart relationships. Instead of accepting responsibility for one's anger, people tend to justify the anger they feel. The recipient of one's anger outburst, in most cases, tends to blame themselves for the cause of it instead of getting out of that kind of relationship.

Even in the Bible in Psalm 7:11, we hear, God is a just judge, and God is angry with the wicked every day." Are we surprised that our God can be angry? In James 1:19–21, we are reminded,

> So then my beloved brethren, let every man be swift to hear, slow to speak, slow to wrath, for the wrath of man does not produce the righteousness of God. Therefore, lay aside all filthiness and overflow of wickedness, and receive with meekness the implanted word, which is able to save your souls.

It is not easy to let go of anger. Anger held within only leads to a buildup of resentments. Give anger over to the Lord. Let Him heal you and rid you of anger issues. He is there for you each and every day. He will grant you release if only you will allow Him. In conclusion, in Psalm 19:14, we read,

> LET THE WORDS OF MY MOUTH AND THE MEDITATION OF MY HEART BE ACCEPTABLE IN YOUR SIGHT, O LORD, MY STRENGTH AND MY REDEEMER.

Don't allow your anger to separate you from the Father!

Christ's First Coming

The true meaning of Christ's first coming—*advent*—with Latin roots means "coming." Christians of earlier generations spoke of "the Advent of our Lord." Advent designates a period before Christmas when Christians prepare for the celebration of Jesus's birth. The practice may have begun in some communities as early as the late fourth century.

There are so many things to distract one's attention during the Advent season that we have a tendency to miss the true meaning of Christmas. The worldly society links Christmas with decorated trees, sentimental carols, and parties. So often the real, eternal meaning of Christ's advent is lost, sometimes in people being so occupied with candy and carols, tinsel, toys, and gifts than to give thanks for the real meaning of the holiday—*the birth of our Lord and Savior of the world, Jesus Christ.*

Christmas often involves spending money people don't have for things they really don't need. The season should not be about how much money you spend or the biggest gift you give. Through His birth, we should realize His coming was to save the world and wash away the sins of all nations, and with His spilled blood all who sought after Him could be free and have everlasting salvation with the Father in heaven.

The average American uses up countless numbers of Christmas wrappings ribbons and bows for gifts. All this is in stark contrast to the birth that took place in Bethlehem two thousand years ago. Christians should be thankful He was born for the sake of our future. Remember: *the reason for the season—Jesus*! Heavenly Father, thank You for Your Son. No matter what, He is the best gift of all.

Why Jesus Came

Jesus came to put away sin and give hope to the hopeless. Jesus was manifested to take away our sins, as the apostle John assures us,

> But you know that He appeared so that He might take away our sins. (1 John 3:5)

In the first epistle of Paul to Timothy, Paul writes,

> This is a faithful saying and worthy of all acceptance, that Christ Jesus came into the world to save sinners, of whom I am chief. (1 Timothy 1:15)

Jesus Christ came to earth as the Baby of Bethlehem primarily to die so that He might later become the Christ of Calvary. The standard which the Father demands is that all humans have sinned. Every one of us has fallen short of the glory of God. Between us and the Father, our sins separate us. The separation between the Father and us is so wide and so great that none of us, by our own efforts, is able to close the gap. Only through the Holy Spirit of Jesus Christ can you ever close the gulf between us and the Father. Not even through good works can you get any closer to the Father.

It is through Jesus Christ *only* and your belief in Him as your Savior and Redeemer that opens your path to the Father. If you have true repentance for your sin, you will be forgiven. For those who believe, you are on the way to eternal life in the Father through Jesus Christ. May we all find this immortal pathway in our lives by loving the Lord and believing in Him with all our heart and soul.

Trust in the Father

If this world were a perfect world, then there would be perfect people living in it. This world is not perfect by any stretch of the word perfect. Since this world is not a perfect world, we pass through times of overwhelming hopelessness, despair, and feelings of failure. Those people who have the spirit of the Lord within them have the power to overcome such obstacles. You only need to place your trust in the One who can help you through.

The Father will give you the strength you are seeking and will help you through whatever is happening to you in your time of need. For He is a loving, caring, faithful Father to those who seek and love Him. We all feel hopeless at times, but we must remember who we have in our corner backing us up. Whenever we feel overburdened, we can always look to the Father for our strength and encouragement *always*. As believers in Jesus, we have the knowledge that He will never grow tired or weary if we call upon His name.

> Do you not know? Have you not heard?
> The Lord is the everlasting God. The Creator of
> the ends of the earth. He will not grow tired or
> weary and his understanding no one can fathom.
> (Isaiah 40:28)

Our Father in heaven, as the prophet Isaiah states, gives strength to the weary and increases the power of the weak.

> But those who hope in the Lord will renew
> their strength. They will soar on wings like eagles;

they will run and not grow weary; they will walk and not be faint. (Isaiah 40:31)

Place all your hope and trust in the Father and not grow weary!

In the Background

With the Father in the heavens, He designed the whole plan of Jesus Christ's coming to earth—from His birth, His ministry, His messages, His miracles, Gethsemane, Calvary, His tomb, His resurrection, His ascension into heaven, and reception of the Holy Spirit. Through receiving the Holy Spirit, the Church was established with Jesus Christ as the head and our faithful intercessor.

To save more people, the Father did all this for us. The intent of the Father was to have His Word taken into all the world, and it is the work of the Church to do this. The business of the elders is to teach *all things* and to establish new churches.

> Teaching them to observe all things whatsoever I have commanded you. And surely I am with you always, to the very end of the age. (Matthew 28:20)

We should be faithful individuals whose mission is to establish new churches as we have been commanded to do. It should be our desire to obey the Bible and its teachings.

> *And He himself gave some to be apostles, some prophets, some evangelists, and some pastors and teachers. For the equipping of the saints for the work of ministry, for the edifying of the body of Christ.* (Ephesians 4:11–12)

Everything in this world was planned out by our Father in heaven, designed in the background to bring all the faithful to the knowledge of the Father, obeying His commands and receiving all His blessings for those who believe in Him. For He placed His only Son, Jesus Christ, to carry out His plan of salvation for all.

God Is with Us

We all deal with crises at some point in our lives. For some, crises are overwhelming at times—a hurricane, devastating fire, a tragic accident, etc. Crises can become more intimate for others—the death of a loved one, disappointment with a dream, a setback at work, etc. No matter what the crisis is, it can make people feel like God has left them.

If you are feeling all alone, feeling no one cares, don't worry as you are not alone. Fear of abandonment is a common reaction. You may think that you have lost everything, as I can attest to in my own life. "No one can help me now; I have really messed up this time." I soon realized that was not the case. It took me a while, but I have not lost everything; there is someone who can help.

That someone is our Lord and Savior, Jesus Christ. God did not cause your crises to happen. Patiently, He is right beside you, even as you are reading this. He waits and hungers for you to turn to Him. That seems hard to believe, but that is the gospel.

The Bible tells us that a person who turns to the Father shall not be afraid of the evil one. Trusting in the Lord is where your heart should reside. Your trust in the Lord will overcome your crisis, emerging intellectually, emotionally, and spiritually fortified. Always remember that the Father is our refuge and strength, a very present help in trouble. The crisis that you are experiencing now may seem daunting, but the Father will see you through to the end. *Just remember that the Father is with you always!*

The Mystery of Suffering

Both great and small, life is marked by events of suffering. With loss, grief, and sorrow, these are by-products of natural disasters impacting entire communities. Others have a profound effect on the world of human evil. Others, affecting a single family, are intensely private. In the struggle to understand all these cases a common thread appears—why does suffering happen?

The intense suffering of Job can be found in the book of Job. If you read chapter 28, the Father finally speaks to Job. The Father doesn't give answers; He just asks questions. In dumbfounded silence, Job stands before the Almighty Father. He wanted to know "*Why?*" The Father responded "*Who.*" For us, the lesson is that we can trust in the Father. If the Father can run the universe in such a spectacular way, we can trust His love and wisdom with the inexplicable and puzzling mysteries of life.

We do not know what the Father will do in the future for us or for our loved ones who are struggling. This we know for sure: we can trust in Him to pull us through our suffering. Jesus insists that it is the grieving ones who are blessed; it is surprising to hear.

"Blessed are those who mourn," Jesus says. (Matthew 5:4)

Suffering and sorrow will always be a part of life, but that is not what Jesus is saying. Rather, find that the Father's mercy and kindness pour over those who need it the most. Don't lose hope in the mystery of suffering!

In Christ the Lord

Jesus came to earth to destroy the works of Satan once and for all, to never have power over death. In 1 John 3:8 we read,

> The one who does what is sinful is of the devil, because the devil has been sinning from the beginning. The reason the son of God appeared was to destroy the devil's work.

Filled with the good news of the Father is the message that what has been made available to us; all we need to do is ask for the understanding of what we are reading with an open mind. Satan is a liar and a murderer, trying to deceive anyone who will listen to him and his lies. This is the reason Jesus came. The Bible says that He came to destroy the works of Satan and place him in the lake of fire. But that is not the only reason Jesus came. Along with putting Satan in his place, He came to give hope to the hopeless, to bring love to the unlovable, to give salvation to all those seeking the glory of the Father, and to shed His precious blood to cleanse the world of sin.

> The night is nearly over; the day is almost here. So let us put aside the deeds of darkness and put on the armor of light. (Romans 13:12)

Redeeming Love

Redeeming love
The love that Jesus gave
When He was nailed to the cross
That the world could be free!

Jesus paid the price
For our redemption
So we didn't have to.

There is no amount of redeeming love
That *we* could give
That would cover the cost
Of which we owe.

Only the redeeming love
Of our Lord and Savior Jesus
Could ever cover that cost
Which the Father
Had already ordained
Before the beginning of time.

Look to the father
For your *redeeming love*!

The Fact of Sin

This truth is clearly disclosed in the Scriptures. Your salvation involves God as well as you. Every person must face the basic fact as they consider their spiritual relationship to the Father—that of sin. To some extent, every human being is conscious of sin, although some may not want to openly admit it. Almost immediately, when a person wants to pray or turn to the Father in their time of need, the inborn consciousness and unworthiness felt because of sin arise within them.

If you haven't already, you, too, must come face to face with the unalterable fact of sin. As you consider the matter of your salvation between the Father and you, you should become conscious of the wall that is built up through sin. Your conscience, common honesty, along with the convincing voice of the Holy Spirit and the Bible, show you have sinned greatly against the Father.

> We all, like sheep, have gone astray; each of us has turned to our own way; and the Lord has laid on him the iniquity of us all. (Isaiah 53:6)

Dealing with Doubt

Many people deal with doubt and uncertainty on a daily basis, whether it be worldly or spiritual. There are even some who believe a person cannot be assured of eternal life until he or she faces the Father at the judgment seat after death. Some true Christians even believe that it is impossible to achieve such assurance in this life. This is not what the Bible indicates. The message of the gospel in the New Testament doesn't portray the followers of Christ wandering through life in darkness and uncertainty, never sure of their salvation until death.

> FOR GOD SO LOVED THE WORLD THAT HE GAVE HIS ONE AND ONLY SON THAT WHOEVER BELIEVES IN HIM SHALL NOT PERISH BUT HAVE ETERNAL LIFE. (John 3:16)

Whoever believes in the name of Jesus Christ has everlasting salvation through eternity (to the ends of time). Christians can be sure of their salvation. How can we be sure of salvation? Once you accept Jesus in your life and allow Him to dwell in your heart, the Father promised you salvation and eternal life in the name of Jesus.

To deny the promise of the Father of the assurance of salvation would be to deny the message of the good news from the Father, thus insulting the Holy Spirit who inspired John's writing. To doubt that you have eternal life is to say that the Father is untrue to His promise of salvation. Do you not think that it would be reasonable that the

Savior who has asked you to follow Him would not give you assurance of your eternal home?

> I WRITE THESE THINGS TO YOU WHO BELIEVE IN THE NAME OF THE SON OF GOD SO THAT YOU MAY KNOW THAT YOU HAVE ETERNAL LIFE. (1 John 5:13)

Your Kingdom Come

Father, let Your kingdom come
Let Your will be done.
Lord, keep that devil on the run
Gracious Father
Allow him not any fun.
Thank You, Father, for Your Son
Knowing You, Lord
Makes my heart shine as the sun.
Lord Jesus, let Your light shine
To keep me in line.
To me, Lord, You are one of a kind
When You come, Lord
Don't leave me behind.
Open my eyes
Remove that which I am blind.
Lord Father, it is You I seek
For my flesh is weak.
I know now, Father
It is not for me to ask why
But to serve until the day I die.
Don't believe Satan
For he will always lie
Just knock him right in the eye.
For in the middle of my war
It was You, Lord, who took control.
Lord Father, lead me back to Your fold
As I await Your kingdom to come!

Made Alive with Christ

When I was out there in the world, no one could tell me anything. I did as the world did. I was spiritually dead, not physically dead. My sinful nature kept me in sin. For a long time, the Holy Spirit convicted me until one day I couldn't say no, and my whole life changed right before my eyes. The things that I once did, I wanted no part of anymore. All the places I hung out, I ran away from. It was like this magnet pulling me in the opposite direction that my current life was heading.

Now that I have found the grace of the Father, I am made alive in the Spirit of a loving, caring, understanding, and merciful Father. Nevermore to be Satan's slave of evil doings, but to honor the one true Father who sent His one and only Son to shed His precious blood to redeem a sinner like myself and for the whole world. That was a Hallelujah moment for me. It can be one for you also. Stop running and give everything over to the One who went through hell so you didn't have to.

> But God is so rich in mercy and He loved us so much, that even though we were dead because of our sins, He gave us life when he raised Christ Jesus from the dead (It is only by God's grace that you have been saved). For He raised us from the dead along with Christ and seated us with Him in the heavenly realms because we are united with Christ Jesus. (Ephesians 2:4–7)

There is everlasting life with Christ.

The Father or Satan

When faced with a critical illness or a hopeless situation, we have options. We can whine and look for pity, or we can complain, which no one wants to hear in the first place or blame the Father. On the other hand, you can see the crisis as an opportunity to make requests of the Father.

Mary and Martha asked Jesus to help them with their sick brother, Lazarus. Then they gave Jesus the glory for the amazing miracle that He performed by raising their brother Lazarus from the dead. If we can humbly ask the Father for help, we will make progress in our recovery. If He can raise someone from the dead, then He is powerful enough to help us overcome our dependencies and character flaws. The Father is only a prayer away. Put away that foolish pride and join the real world—*the world of joy in being united with the Father.*

Satan has you living where there is only heartache and false pride. The Father gives you hope, happiness, joy, and everlasting salvation. *Now* you choose which life is best for you—*darkness or light.* You can either stay in the world and be Satan's *whipping boy,* or you can come out of the world into the light of the Lord and have everlasting life. The choice is yours to freely make.

> COME UNTO ME, ALL OF YOU WHO ARE WEARY AND CARRY HEAVY BURDENS, AND I WILL GIVE YOU REST. TAKE MY YOKE UPON YOU. LET ME TEACH YOU BECAUSE I AM HUMBLE AND GENTLE AT HEART, AND YOU WILL FIND REST FOR YOUR SOUL. (Matthew 11:28–29)

Which will it be, the Father or Satan?

Inborn Nature

According to the teaching of the Bible, everyone enters the world with an inborn nature that sometimes has the tendency to go astray. That doesn't mean that every child has a disposition to rob banks or mug helpless victims. We are predisposed toward doing wrong. Most of us underestimate the sinfulness of the human heart.

Pride is a big factor in our attitude about life. We sometimes let our pride get ahead of the *horse*, so to speak. When that happens, we seem to get caught up in the world and say and do things that normally shouldn't happen, like the stubbornness of the mind, the lack of genuine love for others, and the distrust of the Father when we face hard places head-on in life. All of us need salvation and deliverance from the guilt and power of sin, whether we want to admit it or not.

The greatest miracle in the Bible is not the parting of the Red Sea or the raising of Lazarus from the dead, but the conversion of an individual by the power of God so that the person becomes a new creature in Christ Jesus. To live evermore in the power of the One who gave us His all by going through all the agony and pain for all the world.

Our inborn nature can be changed. Our trials and tribulations and temptations that we all experience are all washed away by the Father's love for us if only we believe in Him and trust in Him and speak to Him directly.

A Remarkable Life

Jesus's ministry on earth was appointed by God for a special purpose. He had a clear sense of His mission. He taught the church during His lifetime by preaching the truth of the Father with authority. From the bondage of sin, Jesus set people free. That is how much He loved everyone, even those who made fun of Him while He was dying on the cross. He showed great love. Before He died, He asked the Father for forgiveness for everyone who rejected Him. *Forgive them, Father, for they know not what they do!*

The last words He said before He gave up the ghost were, "It is finished." For our sins, He completed His purpose for coming to our rescue on earth. Because of who He is, that's the reason He could do what He did for all sinners of this world—*the One and only Son of God!*

When Jesus came to earth as a human, He came to deal with Satan and sin.

> HE THAT COMETH SIN IS OF THE DEVIL; FOR THE DEVIL SINNETH FROM THE BEGINNING. FOR THIS PURPOSE THE SON OF GOD WAS MANIFESTED, THAT HE MIGHT DESTROY THE WORKS OF THE DEVIL. (1 John 3:8)

In addition, Jesus came to our rescue so that the world's sins could be cleansed, reestablish fellowship with the Father, and teach about the Father. Jesus was the perfect man and the perfect servant of the Father in association and constant fellowship with the Holy Spirit. Get to know the Savior; your life can be remarkable as well.

Your Choice—Eternal Life or Eternal Damnation

In Revelation 20:11–15, we see the final judgment of humankind, also known as the Great White Throne Judgment. The standard by which we will be judged is simple. Our names will be found in the great Book of Life, that is, if you have accepted the Father's wonderful gift of salvation through His Son, Jesus Christ. If we choose that path, we will spend eternity in heaven with the Father.

If we have chosen to reject Christ, then our names will not appear in the Book of Life. Our final destination will be the lake of fire. No arguments. Case closed. No debate. No nothing.

Unwittingly, many people will choose the latter option, sadly to say. They do so not because they want to spend eternity in agony, but just because they go with the flow. Like the saying that I have heard time and again—"Monkey see, monkey do!" Why would you want to go along with what everyone else does when it's your life that is on the line? So many find it easy to follow rather than to lead.

As for me, I don't see it being so easy. My way is to follow in the footsteps of the One who gave me everlasting life of peace, joy, happiness, grace, and love. Makes more sense to me. But who am I? The person who is tired of standing on the outside looking in when I can be right there with the Father and living a life of peace and harmony. *That is I!*

Ambassadors

When you were given salvation by the Father, He also gave you the privilege of going out and leading others to Christ, our redeeming Savior of the world. He has chosen you to be His ambassador, which is the greatest privilege ever to be given by the Father. We have been reconciled by Jesus to the Father, and He has given unto us the ministry of reconciling others to Him.

> NOW THEN, WE ARE AMBASSADORS FOR CHRIST, AS THOUGH GOD DID BESEECH YOU BY US, WE PRAY YOU IN CHRIST'S STEAD, BE YE RECONCILED TO GOD. (2 Corinthians 5:20)

As ambassadors for Christ, it is both a privilege and a responsibility to all believers, the ministry of reconciliation urging everyone to come into the right relationship with the Father. The only way that nonbelievers are going to know about the salvation and graces of the Father, or even be saved, is by believers sharing the truth about how the Savior became the light of happiness in their lives.

To really enjoy the Christian life is to join in the work of soul-winning. He that winneth souls is wise in the eyes and ways of the Father. Through this work of sharing the gospel message with others, we show that we are true children in the family of the Father and sole heirs to the kingdom of God.

The fruit of the righteous is a tree of life. To every Christian, some gift or ability to witness to others Jesus Christ has already given. Heavenly Father, thank You for making all believers Your ambassadors to spread Your Word. Give us the power and strength to uphold Your glorious name!

The Loneliest Man

I once considered myself the loneliest man. I felt as if I was all alone in the world of so many. No one seemed to care for me. I had no friends to speak of, and the ones I had were only my friends as long as I could provide for them what I had—drugs and alcohol.

As a child, I was always alone even when there were brothers to confide in. It was like something inside of me didn't want me to have anyone that I could trust. Each time someone would try to reach out to me, I would always push them away for some reason I can't explain. Even as a grown-up, I always felt alone; something was missing. Not until I came to prison did I finally realize what my problem was. It was the lack of love that allowed me to wander around with these feelings of unwantedness and lack of caring by others.

Then one day, while feeling down and out, I heard a voice speaking to me. I thought this is it; you have finally gone over the edge and they will soon be coming to put me in a straitjacket, taking me away to the *funny farm*. That voice said to me, "I have your back. There is someone who loves you very much and you are not going to any *funny farm*. Just let go and trust in Me, for I will not ever forsake you or abandon you."

Now I can see the light and truly know that I am loved. So my brethren, when you have that mistaken identity of not being loved, you are loved more than you will ever know. The Savior loves you and don't ever forget that.

Think of how Joseph must have felt when his own brothers first threw him in a deep pit and then sold him to a group of Ishmaelites who then took him to Egypt. Would Joseph have felt alone and unwanted in addition to being scared, and not knowing where his life was leading? Even later, he was thrust into prison on false charges.

In conclusion, don't ever think that you are the loneliest person on earth. You may not have the support of your family, but there is One who loves you so much that He died for you. If that isn't love, then I don't know what is. *There is no loneliest man; Jesus is love!*

The Meaning of the Cross

Jesus' death was no accident. His death was at the very heart of the Father's plan for His Son. Through the death of the Father's Son, salvation was brought into the world. For our sins, Jesus willingly gave His life as a sacrificial payment for the sins of the world. Before the Father even created the world, Jesus's death had been planned. For our sins to be cleansed and for the ransom for our sins, Jesus was crucified. There would be no salvation from sin without His death but only sorrow, pain, worry, and unhappiness. There would be no joy, no hope. The major theme of worship in heaven is the death of our Savior, Jesus.

By dying for our sins, Jesus would receive from the Father the judgment that we deserved.

> All we like sheep have gone astray; we have turned everyone to his own way; and the Lord hath laid on Him the iniquity of us all. (Isaiah 53:6)

> For Christ also suffered once for sins, the just for the unjust, that He might bring us to God, being put to death in the flesh but made alive by the Spirit. (1 Peter 3:18)

> For He made Him who knew no sin to be sin for us, that we might become the righteousness of God in Him. (2 Corinthians 5:21)

Thank you, holy and righteous Father, for the giving of Your Son, Jesus Christ, as the Savior of the world. In the name of Jesus, *amen*!

Mouth Sins Are Not Trivial

Jesus warned that our words are so important that they will actually determine our condemnation or our justification. Somehow *mouth sins* have been domesticated and entertained unfortunately by the modern church. Gossip, backbiting, and slander are serious habits. Paul even addressed these bad-mouthers when he wrote to the church at Rome stating that these actions were in the same league as murderers, sexual perverts, and haters of the Father. Furthermore, he said such sins are worthy of a death sentence. Read Romans 1:28–32.

Because of their *mouth sins*, some believers have experienced problems and misfortunes or failed to get answers to their prayers. To ridicule and gossip about our brothers and sisters is clearly sin and, as we know, unrepented sin cuts off the flow of the Father's answers to our prayers.

> If I regard iniquity in my heart, the Lord
> will not hear. (Psalm 66:18)

Of those whose mouths are undisciplined and are used for wickedness, Satan takes advantage and uses that for his wickedness.

> Whoever guards his mouth and tongue
> keeps his soul from trouble. (Proverbs 21:23)

The Bible teaches those who will live righteously that they, who desire to dwell in the presence of the Father, to experience His blessings, are those who will not backbite or badmouth their neighbor.

Furthermore, the Father promises a long blessed life to those who keep their tongue from evil.

> Who is the man who desires life, and loved many days, that he may see good? Keep your tongue from evil and your life from speaking deceit. (Psalm 34:12–13)

Mouth sins condemn!

God Is with Us

Crisis, no matter the size, can make people feel like the Father has abandoned them for some reason or other. They wonder how it could be happening to me. *Where is God when I need His understanding and wisdom for what I am going through?*

If you are feeling that way right now, don't worry. You are not alone in what you are experiencing. When we plow through our little valleys, it is only natural that we feel all alone and that we are not going to find our way out.

Well, I have good news for you. The Father hasn't abandoned you. For Jesus said that He will not leave you nor forsake you. When you begin thinking that way, it only makes it easier for Satan to further place doubt in your mind. So don't give him any ground to get at you. Put your trust in the Father, for He is working everything out for your good.

What sometimes angers me is that we claim to love and trust in the Father to take care of all our troubles, but yet, when we get into a crisis, our faith seems not to be as strong as when everything was going well. We start doubting the powers of the Father to guide us through the crisis.

Even so, sometimes we have to trod our way through some trial or tribulation to make us strong. Life can't be a bed of roses all the time. Sometimes we need to be pricked by the thorns on that rose to wake us up to appreciate that rose bed, to really appreciate life and what the Lord Jesus has done for us, even though we are not deserving of His love. Life can be very cruel at times. If life was always easy, then we wouldn't need the Father, but without the Father, we would have no purpose. Life without purpose is useless. *Don't go through life feeling all alone, for you have a purpose, and God is there with you always!*

Fear Not

Have no fear
Jesus will make it clear

He is very near
And your life He wants to steer

Holding your life to Him dear
To you, it may not seem to appear

Listen for His voice
When whispering in your ear
Ask the Father for your heavenly gear

There is a time for sorrow
And there is a time to cheer

Reach out and have no doubt
That the Father has all the power and clout

Jesus Lives Forever

The Father's plan of salvation, along with Jesus's death and resurrection, began a new era in the lives of the people in the world for time and eternity. What His resurrection accomplished is of great significance to the world.

It seemed as though when Jesus died, the evil of the world was in control. Yet on that Sunday morning, three days later, a far superior power had taken over. The Father had acted to show the world that He was yet in control of events all the time. Nothing changed except now the world had a Savior, someone to pay the ransom for all our sins. The Father acted with a power that overcame the Roman guards at the tomb holding Jesus's body. Not for long! The stone was rolled away, a great earthquake occurred, and from the grip of death, Jesus was set free to overcome death forever.

By raising His Son from death, the Father gave great honor to His Son.

> TO YOU FIRST, GOD HAVING RAISED UP HIS SERVANT JESUS, SENT HIM TO BLESS YOU, IN TURNING AWAY EVERY ONE OF YOU FROM YOUR INIQUITIES. (Acts 3:25)

The Father reversed the plan of Satan, the Jewish, and the Roman authorities. Over all demonic powers, the Resurrection placed Christ in a position of authority.

> *Which He wrought in Christ when he raised Him from the dead, and set Him at His own right hand in the heavenly places far above all principality, and power, and might, and dominion, and every*

name that is named, not only in this world, but also in that which is to come. (Ephesians 1:20–21)

Give your life to Jesus and live forever!

Holy Father

Holy Father, good and mighty
All the saints adore Thee
Bless the poor along with me
Trust in the Father
And then you will see
The holes in His hands
Where He was nailed to a tree
To give the world hope
For all of us to be free

There is no one as glorious
In all the world but He
Praise Thy name on earth
And sky and sea
Trust in the Lord
For He is always the same
Believe in the Lord
And you won't go down in fame
Your salvation you can claim
Of the Father be not ashamed
You great and holy Father!

Mistakes in Life

Everyone makes
Mistakes in life
But that doesn't mean
They have to pay for them
The rest of their lives
Sometimes good people
Make bad choices
Which doesn't mean
They're bad
It means they are human
Heavenly Father
O honest one
O honorable one
Purity without sin
Everlasting life
Forgiver of sins
Our Savior and Redeemer

Life-Changing

There is nothing
Quick or easy
About walking with God
But there is something
Life-changing!
As you walk
With Christ Jesus
Living out the faith
He supplies
He continues
To bring you
To points of repentance
Forgiveness
And peace
To places of power
And service
To deposits
Of the deep strength
Provided by love!
They that wait upon the Lord
Shall walk, and not faint.
(Isaiah 40:31)

Jesus's Return to Heaven

The final event in Jesus's earthly life was His ascension into heaven. Before Jesus ascended to heaven after His resurrection, He lived on earth for forty days. He didn't live with His disciples as before His death. During this time, however, He did appear to them often.

> To whom also showed Himself alive after His passion by many infallible proof, being seen of them forty days, and speaking of the things pertaining to the kingdom of God. (Acts 1:3)

As He had promised, He gave proof to them that He had actually risen. Another purpose that He showed Himself was that He wanted to commission His disciples for their witnessing work. For the coming of the Holy Spirit, He wanted to get them prepared as they shared the Father's message with others. He wanted them to know that they would have the Father's power to lead and help them along their journey.

The Bible records many truths about the Ascension of Christ. His earthly experience was completed by His Ascension up to heaven to be placed at the right hand of the Father in His kingdom. Praise be to You, Lord Jesus Christ!

Paradise

What would you say is the most important thing with which we deal every day? Human desires fit that answer: relationships of some kind. Whether it is seeking wealth and fame, or just going about our daily lives, it always comes back to fulfilling relationships. Man's five senses, which the Father gave when He created humankind, were perfect and could not be used for evil. The newly created man knew nothing about evil.

The information the Father gave man could be used to make decisions, to relate to all kinds of things, and even to form emotional attachments based on that which is discovered. Man's spirit with the Father was created perfectly. God actually walked in the garden with man. It's amazing. To perfectly complement man, woman was created.

Each strengthened the weak points in each other, even though they had physical and emotional differences. To communicate with the Father perfectly, man's spirit was created. This made for companionship to the Father whose design was also to provide fulfillment and companionship for the man and woman as well.

In reading Genesis 1:26–31, we find that God the Father created this great paradise where His creations could thrive amongst the beauty, love, and unity in man and woman's relationship. Everything created was good! The Garden of Eden was much more than a paradise for plants and its atmosphere. It was a perfect paradise of the Father who began His relationship with man and woman the instant they were created. *Thank You, Heavenly Father, for breathing life into me also!*

Bought by Blood

We were bought by the blood
Of our Lord and Savior Jesus Christ
At Calvary and cleansed by His blood
For all our sins
He paid the price
That we could not
Because of our sin-stained soul
On Calvary, He showed us
The way to come to the Father
And be bold about it
In the Gospels of Matthew, Mark, Luke, and John,
The life of our Savior is told
Come to the Lord and make your life whole
The Father will take you out of the cold
And place you in the fold of His loving arms
To walk on streets
Paved with gold
So, my brethren, fall down on your knees
Give the Lord the respect
That He deserves
Praise Him in a mighty way!

The Baptist's Cry

Jesus Christ, the Son of the Father, is Mark's theme—*the Good News*—because his purpose is to emphasize the servant role of the Lord Jesus. All of this was announced by John the Baptist, the herald of the good news of the coming Messiah, after which began the ministry of the Savior.

Before John the Baptist came, both Malachi and Isaiah predicted that a messenger would precede the Messiah, making it known that there would be one coming who said that he wasn't even worthy enough to tie the sandals of his feet, telling the people to get morally and spiritually prepared for His coming.

> *Behold, I send My messenger and he will prepare the way before Me. And the Lord whom you seek, will suddenly come to His temple, even the messenger of the covenant, in whom you delight. Behold, He is coming, save the Lord of hosts.* (Malachi 3:1)

> *The voice of one crying in the wilderness; "prepare the way of the Lord, make straight in the desert" a highway for our God.* (Isaiah 40:3)

In John the Baptist, these prophecies were fulfilled. He was the messenger and the voice which cried in the wilderness for the people to repent to be forgiven of their sins and receive salvation and grace from the Father. *Repentance*—a change of mind and heart.

In its biblical sense, repentance refers to a deeply seated and thoroughly turning from self to God. It occurs when a radical change takes place, an experience in which God is recognized as the most important facet of one's existence.

As the people did repent, John the Baptist baptized them, which represented an outward expression of their about-face. Accepting the Savior to dwell in their hearts and lives forever. It united those who were ready to receive Christ.

Give Your Life to Christ

A worldly man giving up on things is not in our category. It is not part of our structure. We have too much pride to even think along those lines. Many feel it is a sign of weakness. It is an unspoken prison code. But then man's ways are not the Father's ways.

> For my thoughts are not your thoughts,
> neither are your ways my ways saith the Lord.
> (Isaiah 55:8)

That is exactly what the Father is asking us to do. Surrender our lives over to Him. By giving your life over to the Lord, you will find fulfillment in life that you have been looking for in all the wrong places. Only when we come to the end of our self-centered ways will the Father be able to help us and guide us on the right road in our journey for peace and harmony.

> In all thy ways acknowledge Him and He
> shall direct thy path. (Proverbs 3:6)

We will then find our true meaning and purpose in this life of pain and suffering. The Lord doesn't wish anyone to suffer, but to have a spirit-filled life of peace and joy, and love for our enemies and each other.

> For whoever wants to save his life will lose
> it, but whoever loses his life for me will find it.
> (Matthew 16:25)

For the Son of Man is life, and more abundantly, by using our own strength, we think we can overcome Satan and our spiritual foes. It will not work. The only way it can work is to give up self and surrender to the Father. Live your life for the one who gave His life on Calvary so you could live. Surrender to Christ and obtain victory.

Heavenly Father, here I am, a broken soul. I give my life to You. Take and use me for Your glory!

Valentine's Day

Roses are red, violets are blue
Jesus died on the cross
For you and me too
Come to the Lord
Let Him fill your heart
Through and through!
Take that old devil
Throw Him out
Just like an old shoe
Give your heart
To the One who died
The Father will replace
That old heart with one anew
On the wings of a dove
The Holy Spirit flew
Without the Lord
You have no clue
What He can do
Just for *you*
Happy Valentine's Day, Lord
All my love forever!

Spiritual Warfare

Not only are we seemingly at war with ourselves but also with others over this topic. The joy that should characterize the Christian life, some feel, is a gloomy state to live with. Others become filled with pride and self-pity as they dwell on the heavy burdens they are immersed in. This kind of attitude does not promote spiritual health. Spiritual warfare implies the struggles that people experience, and they live in denial and fail to see that it does exist but choose to ignore it, which is not good.

These wrong reactions please Satan and thwart the purposes of the Father in and through us. Our spiritual knowledge is increased as our spiritual horizons are enlarged. We then become more useful to the Father as we step out in obedience and faith to do His bidding. In all the warfare that is currently in progress, it is necessary that we first recognize the reality in which we are at war, of which as humans we are a part.

> Finally my brethren be strong in the Lord, and in the power of His might. Put on the whole armor of God that you may be able to stand against the wiles of the devil. For we wrestle not against flesh and blood, but against principalities, against power, against the rulers of the darkness of this world, against spiritual wickedness in high places. (Ephesians 6:10–12)

Put on the full armor of the Lord and trust that He will see you through until the end. Conquer your spiritual warfare through Him who loved you!

Mighty Lord

Mighty Lord
All-powerful and loving
It was the Lord
That calmed the raging sea
Made the winds be still
Holy Lord, You made me
See how much You loved me
Heavenly Father
You hold the key to my heart
You gave me a brand-new start
Out of dust, You made me
From You, Lord
I will never part!

Searching for Wisdom

What is wisdom? The dictionary explains that it is the quality of being wise, and capable of making sound judgments based on your knowledge, experience, and understanding of the situation you are facing. So it is in the spiritual world. The Father is the beginning of all wisdom. When we study the history of redemption, many books in the Bible can be called wisdom literature. There are many styles and types of this literature found in the Bible, which contains good information when we are trying to understand it. It is very helpful to pay close attention to what style that piece of writing concerns. We know that, for example, a sports magazine and a history book are written from different viewpoints, so we read them differently to receive wisdom and understanding.

We should read Proverbs in the same way, differently than Genesis, for example. The book of Proverbs, along with Ecclesiastes, Song of Songs, Job, and Lamentations, speaks of wisdom literature. It talks about this world that is filled with all kinds of sin and about how to get along well in this mixed-up society in which we live, how to worship the Father and honor His will with our actions, words, and thoughts. Wisdom literature shows you all that.

Wisdom is something everyone needs but many do not have. Where does it come from? Proverbs 2:6 tells us,

> The Lord gives wisdom and from His
> mouth come knowledge and understanding.

Everyone should study the wisdom literature of the Bible more to understand the Father's wisdom—the only true wisdom. As fleshly and worldly beings, we are naturally foolish, even from birth. From birth, we are born into sin. To follow the way of wisdom, the Father will teach us. Because we are so unwise to what the Father wants for us is the reason we find ourselves in trouble.

> My goal is that they may be encouraged in heart and united in love, so that they may have the full riches of complete understanding, in order that they may know the mystery of God, namely Christ in whom are hidden all the treasures of wisdom and knowledge. (Colossians 2:2–3)

Stay Calm

Often we find ourselves terribly anxious after a crisis, unable to think or function in a constructive way. Some look at that as *mind over matter*. Simply, we are thinking the wrong thoughts. You should take some time out to drain those tense thoughts and replace them with thoughts of peace, calmness, and faith. For example, open your Bible to Psalm 23, read it aloud, and concentrate on the message therein.

By seeking the Father's wisdom, you will be lifted and strengthened if you are sincere. When you pray to the Father, ask Him to take worrisome thoughts and replace them with healthy thoughts, and receive His grace which passes all understanding. At times, life can deal some chilling blows. But the Father yearns to heal us from the sadness of this sinful world if only we would let Him.

Then we must remember feelings of sorrow are nothing of which we should be ashamed. When you feel overwhelmed with sorrow, find your way to the Father and seek His calming grace to heal your wounded heart. Remember also that you are bigger than anything that comes your way. While acting in the spirit of the Lord Jesus Christ, you will gain the power to be healed and receive His calming graces.

Stay in the power of our Lord and Savior Jesus Christ and be calm!

Cleansed Completely

That wily devil
No longer
Has a hold on me
For the Lord broke in
And set me free
There are no more shackles
On my feet
Hallelujah!
The Lord has made me complete
Causing that old devil to flee
And no more, Lord,
Can they nail You to a tree
You went down
Took back that which Satan
Stole from Thee
You then opened up
The eyes of the world
So they may see
With the Father
Is the only place to be
Thank You, Lord, for completely cleansing me!

The Invisible Battle

There is an invisible battle going on inside us all. It is like no war that you've ever heard of outside the body. The war that I am talking about is the war between the spirit and Satan. If you don't have the power of the Holy Spirit on your side, the war with Satan has already been won, for the human body cannot stand up against his demonic powers. An invisible curtain hides this warfare that is happening between the flesh and the Holy Spirit.

This is not a foreign worldly war that touches us very closely. Everyone who is saved and born again is allied with the Father. For those who are not, now is the time to get your life in order with the Father before it's too late. We are not promised a tomorrow. You can't say, "I will do it tomorrow." The enemy we have met is ourselves; we are our own worst enemy. The Father wants to have a relationship with us, but it is we who must make the first move and ask Him to come into our lives.

Even at times when we struggle because of the effect of living in a broken world, we have a Father who loves us not begrudgingly, but with rejoicing, lasting love that *endures forever*. We ultimately have the choice to remove this invisible barrier and glory in the Father.

Doers of the Word

In analyzing the scriptures in the Bible, the reader should realize how important the truths within are in the Christian walk. Unless you allow the word in which you are studying to change your life, a person cannot consider himself a good student of the word. Therefore, for the word to grasp that person, he or she has to grasp it.

James said it well when he wrote,

> But be doers of the word, and not hearers only, deceiving yourselves. For if anyone is a hearer of the word and not a doer, he is like a man observing his natural face in a mirror; for he observes himself, goes away, and immediately forgets what kind of man he was. But he who looks into the perfect law of liberty and continues in it, and is not a forgetful hearer but a doer of the work; this one will be blessed in what he does. (James 1:22–25)

Scriptural truth, when put into practice in your life, will make you stronger, especially when shared with others. Through sharing the word, understanding can be absorbed and retained, reminding one to always seek after what is good and righteous for his or her own life. In addition, it will also encourage a person to become stronger in their study of the Bible.

Heavenly Father, give me the strength not only to be a hearer of Your word but a doer as well, to give You all the glory!

Sowing and Sharing

> *Whoever sows to please their flesh, from the flesh will reap destruction; whoever sows to please the Spirit, from the Spirit will reap eternal life.* (Galatians 6:8)

We must plant seeds to bring a harvest. Whatever we sow, we also will reap, the Bible tells us. If we plant corn, we reap corn, not peaches. If we plant apple trees, we will reap apples, not oranges. In all areas of life, this principle of sowing and reaping is consistent no matter how you look at it.

The more you sow, the more you reap. When you sow good, you reap good. When you sow evil, you reap evil in return. By sharing the word of the Father, you are sowing the good news of Him, and the grace of salvation awaits those who allow the seeds to grow in their hearts. If we as believers continue to share the word of the Father with others, we can be certain that our sharing will produce good fruit.

To give our faith to others is the greatest act of sharing and shows obedience to the Father.

> *But I gave them this command: Obey me and I will be your God and you will be my people. Walk in obedience to all I command you, that it may go well with you.* (Jeremiah 7:23)

Remember, God wishes us to sow His Word to mankind to bring about good in the world. Those little seeds you may have planted in the mind of someone, you never can know the influence you may have had in that person's life. A small seed has the ability, if watered and cared for, hopefully will produce welcome fruit. Share Christ with someone today, and the Father will bless you abundantly.

Father, Cleanse Me

> But we are like an unclean thing, and all our righteousness are like filthy rags; we all fade as a leaf, and iniquities like the wind have taken us away. (Isaiah 64:6)

Scripture says something about self-cleansing. All of our efforts at dealing with this issue while we try it on our own, we fall short of our goal. For example, the Israelites never really experienced God's salvation.

> You come to the help of those who gladly do right, who remember your ways, but when we continued to sin against them you were angry. How then can we be saved? (Isaiah 64:5)

Through the grace of the Father, there is always hope. You, Lord, are our Father, who is the potter, and we are just the clay. Our Lord will shape you into a faithful servant if only you will let Him.

All the smudges and smears of sin on our souls we cannot scrub away. Only the blood of Christ Jesus will ever make us free and wash us clean and whole. Thankfully, we can receive salvation in the one whose sacrifice allows us to be cleansed completely.

> But if we walk in the light, as he is in the light, we have fellowship with one another, and the blood of Jesus, His Son, purifies us from all sin. (1 John 1:7)

Thank You, Father, for Your cleansing power!

Life after Death

There is life after death for the believers who are filled with the Holy Spirit of our Lord and Savior Jesus Christ. For followers of the Lord Jesus Christ, death should hold no fear. But for the unsaved, the nonbelievers, physical death leads to eternal torment in hell. This is why the Father has paved the way for salvation for those who seek Him. He sent His Son to bridge the gap that sin had caused. Now there is no excuse for sin unless you choose that path all the while condemning your family as well as yourself.

The Father does not wish that anyone should perish but should come to repentance and ask for forgiveness. The Father is a just and forgiving Father. When someone dies, we often hear someone say, "Now he or she is in a better place." We believe that those who are saved, yes, he or she is in a better place, for they will be in heaven with the Lord for eternity.

What about the nonbeliever? Those who never took the time to really get to know the Father (the unsaved) will fall into a far worse place than they were before death. They never realized what the Father could do in their lives. For we know in Revelation that if your name is not in the Book of Life, you will be cast into the lake of fire, and that is the end of you.

Thank You, Father, for *life* after death! I believe in You wholeheartedly as my Lord and Savior! Come into my heart, for I desire to live with You for all eternity!

Walking with God

When you walk with the Father in truth and light, the Father loves you, and if you love Him, He will deny you nothing.

> *No good thing does (God) withhold from those whose walk is blameless.* (Psalm 84:11)

For the material things of this world, God does not hold against us, but when those material things cause us to turn away from Him, we lose sight of what is most important in our lives—*our salvation.*

One cannot serve two masters. Either you worship the Father or the things of the world. By loving the Father, you will accomplish much more through His love than the treasures of the world. Living in the world is only temporary. When your life here on earth is over, you cannot take anything with you. What you think you have treasured here is no more, all left behind.

However, when the Father becomes your master, and you give your life over to Him, not only do you have everlasting life, but you also become coheirs with the Lord Jesus. You are accepted into a holy family of the Father, which is more beneficial than anything you could ever imagine. The world only leads you to pain, sorrow, and destruction. When the Father gives you life after death, what about it? Are you walking with the Father or the world?

Satan's Methods

To control the lives of people, Satan uses a variety of methods. His wiles are deadly. For the Christian to overcome these deceptive strategies, which appear seemingly harmless on the surface, the believer must enter the battle with their eyes wide open resist any temptations that may occur, and understand the methods employed by Satan for their faith to remain strong.

Concerning our attitude toward Satan, the Bible gives us some very clear and strong instructions. In 1 Peter 5:8,9, we read,

> BE ALERT AND OF SOBER MIND. YOUR ENEMY THE DEVIL PROWLS AROUND LIKE A ROARING LION LOOKING FOR SOMEONE TO DEVOUR. RESIST HIM, STANDING FIRM IN THE FAITH, BECAUSE YOU KNOW THE FAMILY OF BELIEVERS THROUGHOUT THE WORLD IS UNDERGOING THE SAME KIND OF SUFFERING!

Exercise self-control. Be watchful, for it is not simply looking around to see if the enemy (Satan) is near, for we will not see him. The way to be protected and watched is through the Word of the Father so that when Satan casts his fiery darts and seeks to trap us in his wiles, we will be protected by the Word of the Father. Walk with the Father throughout the day. Read the Word and discover what the Lord expects of you. This way, you will be applying the protection of His blood (Jesus) that will keep you from Satan's evil designs. Live your life by the Father's methods and throw out the methods of the evil one!

Praying in Difficult Times

Everyone goes through difficult times in life. Whoever says they don't is not being truthful, not only to themselves but to other people. It doesn't have to be anything major to cause you to consider it to be a difficult situation. Even the smallest things can cause disruption and lead you to think that no one hears your cries during times of great stress.

What is worst of all, sometimes we feel that the Father Himself doesn't listen or hear our cries of pain or see our tears. But He does. The Father sees and hears everything each time one of His children is in a state of anguish. Through prayer to the Father, it is a for sure certain and consistent way to stay in fellowship at all times.

He (God) just doesn't sit around in heaven and look down on His people and not know what we are going through. He is busy at work providing for our every need. His goodness and faithfulness are a way of affirming the Father's sovereignty.

In Psalm 61, David brings his petitions before his Creator, stating,

> From the ends of the earth, I cry to you for help when my heart is overwhelmed. Lead me to the towering rock of safety, for you are my safe refuge, a fortress where my enemies cannot reach me. (Psalm 61:2–3)

Pray in difficult times; the Father surely will hear you and answer you!

The Christian's Armor

To enjoy full victory against the devil, we must put on the whole armor of God. In Ephesians 6, the spiritual armor and the description of the armor that the followers of Christ Jesus have been given to protect people in this fierce combat with the enemy (Satan) and his armies.

> THEREFORE, PUT ON EVERY PIECE OF GOD'S ARMOR SO YOU WILL BE ABLE TO RESIST THE ENEMY IN THE TIME OF EVIL. THEN AFTER THE BATTLE YOU WILL STILL BE STANDING FIRM. STAND YOUR GROUND PUTTING ON THE BELT OF TRUTH AND THE BODY ARMOR OF GOD'S RIGHTEOUSNESS. FOR SHOES, PUT ON THE PEACE THAT COMES FROM THE GOOD NEWS SO THAT YOU WILL BE FULLY PREPARED. (Ephesians 6:13–15)

Remember, the whole armor of the Father enables us to stand on our own two feet prepared for when that evil day comes. To wait until that day arrives may be too late. We must be prepared to stand against the wiles of Satan.

Just because the Savior has beaten Satan when He went to the cross and resurrected doesn't mean that Satan has given up. He is a very stubborn and prideful foe—a defeated foe. But you can't let your guard down at any time for he is cunning and sly like a fox. We face an enemy who has been called the Father of Lies, the embodiment of deceit.

John speaks of this in his gospel as he relates a testimony that Jesus admonishes His people,

> FOR YOU ARE THE CHILDREN OF YOUR FATHER THE DEVIL AND YOU LOVE TO DO THE EVIL THINGS HE DOES. HE WAS A MURDERER FROM THE BEGINNING. HE HAS ALWAYS HATED THE TRUTH, BECAUSE THERE IS NO TRUTH IN HIM. WHEN HE LIES IT IS CONSISTENT WITH HIS CHARACTER FOR HE IS A LIAR AND THE FATHER OF LIES. (John 8:44)

To know Christ more intimately, a daily devotional in the Word is so vital for the Father's Words to be understood. Daily devotionals are our source for knowing the truth. In John 14:16, Jesus stated,

> I AM THE WAY, THE TRUTH, AND THE LIFE.

The Word of the Father is our life. Heavenly Father, thank You for Your Word and for Your full armor to protect me in this battle in life. Amen!

Handling Sorrow

We as humans handle our sorrow in many different ways. Some turn to alcohol, drugs, self-pity, and remorse. Our minds can become stressed and our souls in anguish. Relief for our condition seems far off. Possibly abandonment, rejection, or despair over the loss of a loved one substantially weighs upon our minds leaving us feeling lost and drowning in sorrow. When will this end?

You think, why did this happen to me? We feel that we are the only person who is experiencing these feelings. Our loss of a loved one hurts so much. One thing that we have to remember is that the physical body dies, but the soul does not. Therefore, we place the blame on the Father not realizing that God does not make mistakes. He fixes them. He does not do evil; the Father does not wish anything bad to happen to you.

The Bible teaches us,

> He was a man of sorrows and familiar with suffering. He was despised and rejected by mankind a man of suffering and familiar with pain like one whom people hid their faces he was despised and we held him in low esteem. (Isaiah 53:3)

While hanging upon that cross, His soul was in deep sorrow and pain. He went through all that just for us, so we could be saved from sin and Satan. Is He not a loving Savior?

Just think about this when we are experiencing our sorrows; we may think our world is coming to an end like I sometimes have done. But our Lord and Savior took upon Himself His suffering for us just so we didn't have to. Thank You, Father, for Your Son dying for our sins and being there when we need You as we progress through sorrows of our own!

Loving Father

My loving Father
I am sorry for my sins
Father, thank You
For the Lord Jesus
Who took all my sins at Calvary
And washed them clean
In His lifesaving blood
That covered me in His love
I was lost in this dark world
He found me
Bringing me toward the light
I was down on my luck
But He picked me up
Making me whole again
I, once a broken foe
Your Son put me back together
Thank You, Father
For giving me my life back

Sin

You see, my friend
To some people
Sin is their best friend
Sin doesn't care
Who it has as a friend
All it cares about
Is how many souls
It can win over
For the evil one—Satan
The Bible teaches you
All about sin
But there is One
Who died for all our sins
Our Savior
Jesus Christ
For when He knocks
Please let Him in
Before your wretched life
Comes to an end
The Lord Jesus
He knows
No sin

Love for Others

As believers in Christ, there should be love for others in our hearts, even toward our enemies. I know you are thinking, "My enemies? How can we love someone who seemingly without failure appears to stress us out at every turn? Do I really need to like them and love them as well when they show such disrespect all the time?"

When you show love toward an enemy, the effect of your kindness will throw them off. They don't understand how to react to kindness and love. This is probably one of the most difficult things a Christian can do. But the Father expects us to do that, as that is His command that we should love one another, even our enemies.

The best way to defeat your enemy is to show kindness, dignity, love, and respect. Either they find someone else to ply their evil deeds, pick on someone else, or they turn their life over to the Father and become a child of the Father or an enemy of God—their choice.

In Acts 9, we read about a woman named Dorcas (also known as Tabitha) who showed compassion and kindness by providing handmade clothing for the poor—either friend or foe, doing the Lord's will at all times.

Instead of fighting or causing angry feelings to erupt when faced with an enemy, we need to pray for that person that his or her heart will become enamored with the love of the Father. We as individuals need to leave a legacy of love whenever we show graciousness to all, regardless of how they may treat us. Remember, God works in mysterious ways; you may never know how this love will be repaid. We are the stronger ones who live in the love of the Father.

Is Satan Still at Large?

Absolutely! In the actions of people, Satan's presence makes a tremendous difference in the world. You can witness this at the present. Satan has access to heaven as well as earth. Evil continues to increase in the world, even though the craftiness of Satan's powers has been limited by the Father. He continually roams the earth as he pleases, moving from one place to another like a snake.

We must not ever forget to put our faith in the Father for our protection. Every type of lewd and violent act imaginable, man is committing without giving any thought to the outcome.

The earth will experience a period of peace and righteousness when Satan will be chained up in time. That time has not existed since the fall of man. For all those who live the rules of Satan and who have brushed aside the Lord's warnings will be judged and will come up short of the Father's grace and salvation. They will begin to wonder why the Savior says to them, "Depart from Me, you workers of iniquity, for I know you not." Imagine how they will feel being rejected by the one who gave Himself so that we wouldn't have to experience that.

The Father works all testing for the good of those who follow Him, though Satan intends such testing for evil. Is Satan still at large? By and far, so be it. He sneaks into our lives when we least expect it. He loves to cause confusion in our lives and loves the weak and powerless. It is up to us not to allow Him entrance into our hearts. We can defeat him so that he will not take charge of Earth and remain at large for long! We as Christians have the power of our Lord and Savior to fight this inhuman being.

Doctrinal Statement

There are three manifested persons in the unity of the Father—God the Father, God the Son (Jesus Christ), and God the Holy Spirit. This we call the Trinity. The Bible is the only true verbally inspired word of the *Father* to humankind. It is, therefore, the sole authority without error for Christian faith and conduct. We believe there is only one true God who is all-powerful and Creator of the universe. Of all honor, love, praise, and glory, He is worthy of all.

We believe that *Jesus* fulfilled all the prophecies concerning the promised Messiah. He (Jesus) was manifested as the Father yet was born of a virgin in the flesh. Through the grace of the Father, Jesus is salvation to all who seek the living water of the Lord Jesus.

The *Holy Spirit*, we believe, is of our Lord and Savior Jesus Christ whose main purpose, if we want to accept the Lord as number one in our lives, is to guide and lead us in our walk with the Father. He, the Spirit, is our teacher, prayer partner, and helper of all to lead godly lives.

We also believe in the Resurrection of our Lord and Savior Jesus Christ. Christians know that through His death and resurrection, and rising from the dead on the third day, we will be saved if we have sincere belief in Christ. We know that all who do not believe are lost into eternal damnation throughout all eternity.

Thank You, loving Father, for Your Son Jesus Christ whom I believe wholeheartedly died on the cross for my sins and was buried and rose again upon the third day.

My Jesus

My Jesus, all-powerful and caring
More than anyone I know
He hung on the cross
So that we may go free
So the world
Could have all their sins
Washed away
In the blood of the Lamb
What a man He must be
My Jesus was sinless
When He was born
Even later having
Been brutally scorned
Then my Lord Jesus
Was sentenced to die
For crimes that were lies
He died there, hanging on that cross
For all the world to see
For sinners far and wide
He rose again
To show the world
His power over death
And you can have it too
The Lord is our salvation
When the Lord knocks on the door to your heart
Let Him in and fellowship with Him
The Lord is your salvation in this wicked and sinful world

Along with salvation is everlasting life
A free gift from the Father
For all who seek it
Hallelujah! That is my Jesus

Choices

Decisions, decisions, decisions! Such is life. Are we like the ostrich who hides his head in the sand, or are we the people who will decide on a course that we want our life to take? The *Oxford Dictionary* defines *choice* as "deciding possibilities." Each day, every one of us makes numerous choices, whether they are good choices or bad ones. Yet they are choices, some being simple, others more difficult. For example, do I want to eat a hamburger or a hot dog today at Dairy Queen? Should I wear this or that outfit to a party I am attending? Which movie will I want to see? These choices, even so simple, can be decided upon without too much trouble, having no long-term effects.

How about high school? Do I want to finish or drop out? As a teenager, shall I join a gang or go it alone? As you can see, these last two choices affect your future, having a greater impact on your life. There may arise many more difficult choices that we as humans will face in our lifetime. However, there is one choice or decision that has an even greater impact on our lives.

That decision is whether to sincerely ask Jesus to be your Savior and become an integral part of your life. The worst thing you can do is not make that decision at all. This important decision will become your true destiny with the Father. He awaits your choice to either follow Him or not.

Be not like the ostrich who hides his head in the sand. Make a firm decision to seek the love of the Father and His goodness and mercy. Make Him the greatest choice in the world. Life is full of choices. We just have to make the right ones! He is waiting. Do you hear His call?

Rest in Jesus

Even with wealth and success, the restless soul is never satisfied. It is always looking for something that is missing. Even with all the achievements that have been made, there is still a restlessness in the soul that you just can't seem to conquer—impulse buying, thinking, *I just need that new dress or suit*, or *I need that new car, or money and finances to make us happy*, or *Our neighbor seems to have this or that*, etc., thinking that what we want will bring us happiness and peace of mind. All too soon, we realize that what we may have just purchased will bring us only temporary happiness, for it will not be long before we crave something else that we claim will bring us happiness. It seems that all we try to do doesn't change the outcome. There is but one thing that will fix everything we have been looking for—*fulfillment*.

Jesus is the one you need to seek after. He invites all those who have become weary from toiling in sin and its consequences to come to Him personally. In the gospel of Matthew, we read,

> Come unto Me all you who are heavy laden, and I will give you rest; Take My yoke upon you and learn from Me, for I am gentle and lowly of heart, and you will find rest for your souls. For My yoke is easy and My burden light. (Matthew 11:28–30)

For the abundant life He provides, the only requirement is to believe in Him and then learn from Him how to live. Jesus doesn't abbreviate our accountability to the Father. He will give us peace to our restless souls, a less burdensome way to live in Him. Holy Father, I come to you for rest and peace of mind forever in You.

My Pet Raccoon

When my father was walking in the woods one day behind our house, he saw a baby raccoon fall into the river. He rescued him and brought him home to be taken care of. He became my pet. He was a smart little critter and he and I had many good times together. Then one day he went missing which brought much sadness to me. My father warned that one day that may happen and turn on you. He belonged to the wild. So my raccoon did just that—ran off turning on me.

Consider in our lives how often we have been harboring *pet* grudges in our lives that are hard to get rid of. We cling to our bitterness despite warnings from the Father to reconcile, seek forgiveness, and restore relationships. Unconfessed sins in our lives will affect our eternal destiny. Many are held in bondage by personal sins. We live with our *secrets* hoping no one will find out.

Our sins will rob us of spiritual vitality making spiritual growth and victory impossible.

> Behold all souls are Mine; the soul of the Father as well as the soul of the Son is Mine; the soul who sins shall die. (Ezekiel 18:4)

What does this have to do with a raccoon? This animal which was meant to be in the wild was taken from its surroundings and tried to make it live in a domesticated world which is against its nature. We harbored it as if it was imprisoned for life. One day, it disappeared and became free to run its own life. Our sins are just like that. We remain captive to live a sinful life, imprisoned so to speak, heavily burdened. By seeking the Father and living a life of reconciliation with Him, the result is *freedom* for us. Isn't that what we should seek?

To Witness

For us to witness to others, the Bible repeatedly emphasizes that it is the duty of followers of Christ to witness to others about the salvation which is ours in Christ Jesus our Savior. In Matthew, the heart of the great commission is "Go and teach."

> Therefore, go and make disciples in all the nations, baptizing them in the name of the Father and of the Son and of the holy spirit, and then teach these new disciples to obey all the commands I have given you; and be sure of this that I am with you always even to the ends of the world. (Matthew 28:19–20)

One form of witnessing is telling people about what the Father has done in your life. Another is by actions by which people can see your joy and love for the Father and the love you show toward others. Witnessing should not be related to door-to-door salesmanship, a wrong approach to soul-winning.

The Father has planted the seeds of witnessing into you; you must then *water* them, and God will grant the increase. It is not the believer's job to save a person. For one thing, we don't have the power to save. Only the Father can save. Your witnessing of your relationship with the Father may just be the impetus for one person to seek salvation. Thank You, Father, for Your trust in me to spread Your lifesaving Word!

This Love Is Real

When a friend of mine found out that the person he loved was cheating on him, he stated that he was ready to give up on life. I counseled him that there was someone who loved him unconditionally. His hurt was so deep he felt that he could never trust again. He couldn't help but wonder if his life would be one disappointment after the other. Will I be hurt again and again?

If you are one who has experienced a similar hurt within a troubled relationship that has left you wary or afraid to trust, you begin to feel the same about the Father's love. Was there a catch to what the Father was saying about how He loves me? I am here to tell you that when He says He loves you, He really means it. In Paul's letter to the Romans, we read,

> But God demonstrates His own love toward us, in that while we were still sinners, Christ died for us. Much more then having now been justified by His blood, we shall be saved from wrath through Him. (Romans 5:8–9)

Dear Jesus, thank You for the great love You showed me when You took on the sins of the world so that everyone could be free to love You in return!

Reflection on Eternity

> For thus says the High and Lofty One who inhabits eternity, whose name is Holy; I dwell in the high and holy place, with him who has a contrite and humble spirit, to revive the spirit of the humble, and to revive the heart of the contrite ones. (Isaiah 57:18)

When loved ones pass on, we wonder where they have gone. Where will that person spend eternity? Hopefully, it will be with the Lord Jesus in heaven, or will that person spend eternity within that lake of fire with Satan?

What is eternity like? For our loved ones we cannot say exactly how things are for them, good or bad. We can only hope for the good, for if they truly love the Lord, they will be all right. As believers, we will see again our loved ones who have passed. What a glorious day that will be! Until that day, come let us be cautious and watchful for even on our deathbed, Satan will buffet us.

Let us not have a fear of death. For death to followers of Christ is sleep and rest until the Savior calls us up to be with Him for all eternity when He returns for all those who belong to Him.

> Therefore submit to God. Resist the devil and he will flee from you. Draw near to God and He will draw near to you. Cleanse your hands, you sinners, and purify your hearts, you double-minded." (James 4:7–8)

When we place our focus on Jesus, we can have victory and power over death. Where do *you* wish to spend eternity? With whom?

The Power of the Word

> For the word of God is living and powerful, and sharper than any two-edged sword, piercing even to the division of soul and spirit, and of joint and marrow; and is a discerner of the thoughts and intents of the heart. (Hebrews 4:12)

When you minister life to people, your words must be anointed with the power of the Holy Spirit. When you speak and minister to the people, your words reflect that of the Holy Spirit which is the same in heaven joined together with the Word of the Father. When you speak the Word of the Father on earth, you are speaking the Word that is in heaven.

The Holy Spirit Jesus promised would come and abide in us to be our helper. He also said that He and the Father would make their home in us if we love Him and keep His Word.

> If you love Me, obey Me; and I will ask the Father and He will give you another comforter, and He will never leave you. (John 14:23)

As you can see, as a believer you have the Trinity living inside of you. That way He (the Holy Spirit) will lead you and guide your steps in your journey, Jesus will save you if you believe in Him fervently, and the Father will always love you the same as He loves His Son.

Heavenly Father, thank You for Your powerful Word for me to use, and thank You for the Holy Spirit to guide my steps! Your Word is my Word!

Lord, Help Me

Lord Father, help me
For I can't do this
On my own
Lord Jesus, I feel all alone
All my spirit
Is gone
I feel like a little dog
Chasing after a bone
It is You, Lord
Who makes me feel strong
Please, Lord,
I don't know
How much longer
I can hold on
I can feel You
In every song
Walk with me, Lord
Then I can't turn wrong
You, Lord, are my cornerstone
It is You, Lord
I want to see
Thank You, Lord
For setting me free
While hanging on that tree!

Bless the Lord

Bless the Lord, O my soul
Bless the Lord and stand bold
Reach out to the Lord
And join His heavenly fold
Be ready to walk the streets of gold
I once was sinking in life's sinking sand
He reached out to me
With His mighty and powerful right hand
Telling me to hold on, my child
For you are in my plan
Walk with me
I will take away all your pain
Bless the Lord in all your ways
For when everyone leaves
You, the Lord, are the One who stays
Honor the Lord with all your days!

Rely on Jesus

When you rely on Jesus
Your life starts to change
The sins you once did
You no longer do
Repent you of all your sins
To the Father
He doesn't keep score
Look to the Father
For you, He opens every door
Tell that devil he is a bore
Watch as his chin falls to the floor
You don't worship him anymore
The Lord is the *guy*
Who stands with open arms
He is the One
Who keeps you from all harm
Rely on Jesus!

My Lord

My Lord is my light
My salvation that shines
Both day and night
Whom shall I fear?
Here Lord, take the wheel
You can steer
When the wicked advance against me
I call out Your name
And watch them flee
You, Lord, they don't want to see
They think they can bully me
But in Your arms, Lord, I feel free
With the Lord Jesus
You can't stumble and fall
The Lord keeps you on the ball
Though an army may besiege me
I have no fear, Lord
You will see me through
When I call
I know You hear my plea!

Spiritual Hunger

We have all experienced physical hunger at times, craving what we want to eat. That feeling of hunger pangs letting us know it's time to eat. Wouldn't it be wonderful if we felt the same pain when seeking spiritual hunger? The removal of sin and its consequences? Finding satiety in the one who freely gives it to us?

> Blessed are those who hunger and thirst for righteousness, for they shall be filled. (Matthew 5:6)

The words that Satan fears most are *spiritual hunger* because the Heavenly Father wants us to be hunger-free for Him. Jesus also hungered for His Father. In His preaching, He spoke only the words that His Father appointed to Him. Jesus only did what He saw His Father do.

> For I have not spoken on my own authority; but the Father who sent Me gave Me a command what I should say and what I should speak. (John 12:49)

Spiritual hunger comes from the Father. His promise to us when we hunger and thirst for Him is that we receive the Holy Spirit to fill us. For the things that are wrong, the Lord wants us to move by the spirit that lives inside each person. In everything you will encounter in this life, spiritual hunger is the catalyst. Many times, we will have to seek the Lord as believers to find answers to our problems. As believers in Jesus, we cannot just believe in the Father and think that is enough to be saved. We at all times must place our hope and trust completely in Him, and He will answer our pleas—have *faith*. In the New Testament, it says,

> But without faith, it is impossible to please Him, for he who comes to God must believe that He is and that He is a rewarder of those who diligently seek Him. (Hebrews 11:6)

Thank you, Father, now that I know who to come to when my spirit hungers!

Brokenness and Humility

> Come to Me all you who labor and heavy laden, and I will give you rest. Take My yoke upon you and learn from Me, for I am gentle and lowly in heart, and you will find rest for your souls. For My yoke is easy and My burden is light. (Matthew 11:28–30)

Many followers of Christ experience brokenness and humility, which are unpopular subjects to consider. In today's culture, people are being told to pump themselves up and be strong emotionally and mentally. The Father, however, wants us to know about these powerful words—brokenness and humility. The Old Testament connects the quality of humility with the Israelites' lowly experience as slaves in Egypt—a poor, afflicted, and suffering people. (Read Deuteronomy 26:6.)

You can see the character of Jesus in Matthew 11:28–30, how He is gentle, lowly, and humble of heart. When you come to the Lord feeling totally broken and down, approach the Lord with humility in your heart, allowing your brokenness of spirit to depart from you and find rest in the Lord. For when it has to do with the Father's discipline, a yoke is good. Jesus tells us for the purpose of our lives, we must take His yoke upon us and learn from Him. To enter the rest of Jesus, you must humble yourself as a broken individual and come to Him in complete submission and obedience. *Come to the Father in brokenness and humility, and He will heal you!*

Saving Grace

Search me, Father
And know my heart
I need a new star
Fill my cup to overflowing
Even the winds listen
To the Lord when blowing
The Lord keeps things steadily flowing
Lord, I need You
In a mighty and powerful way
Take my heart, Father
And mold it like clay
I am thankful to You, Lord
Because of my awful pride
You had to pay
From now on, Lord
To You, I will be faithful
Watching out for that evil Satan
For all his hatefulness
Now that I know You, Father
You always put a smile on my face
Thank You, Father,
For Your saving grace!

The Crucified Life

There is power in the cross. We also know about the power of the Father that caused Jesus to be crucified on the cross. The same power that raised Jesus from the dead. The same power that will also raise you up in the spirit and give you power over the flesh and death. The flesh dies, but the spirit of the Lord Jesus comes and lives in your heart, soul, and mind.

We must yield to the crucified life and walk in the spirit, putting to death the flesh. Satan has no power over the spirit, only the flesh. By living in the flesh, Satan can walk right in and take control. When you live in the spirit of the Savior, he (Satan) has no control.

> For those who live according to the flesh set their minds on the things of the flesh, but those who live according to the spirit, the things of the spirit. For to be carnally minded is death, but to be spiritually minded is life and peace. Because the carnal mind is enmity against God; for it is not subjected to the law of God nor indeed can be. So then, those who are in the flesh cannot please God. (Romans 8:5–8)

> I have been crucified with Christ; it is no longer I who live, but Christ lives in me, and life in which I now live in the flesh I live by faith in the Son of God, who loved me and gave Himself for me. (Galatians 2:20)

When we crucify the life of the flesh, we are raised up in the spirit of Christ!

Heavenly Father

Lord Father in the heavens above
I come to You on this day
Receiving Your graces
Thanking You for Your Son
Jesus Christ and His love
For all the people in this sinful world
Giving You all the praise and honor
In Your Son's name, Jesus Christ
Thank You, Father, for Your love and grace
Thank You for Your mercy
Upon my sinful soul
Thank You for this day
It is a day
You made special in Your sight
Thank You for Your Son
Who took upon Himself
All the sins of the world
Thank You, Father, again
For Your saving grace!

New Life in Christ

Through Jesus Christ, we now have access to the Holy of Holies, and we can freely enter.

> Therefore, brethren, having boldness to enter the Holies by the blood of Jesus by a new and living way which He consecrated for us, through the veil that is His flesh. (Hebrews 10:19–20)

We no longer have to go to the High Priest to have our sins forgiven. Through the life-giving blood of Jesus Christ, which He freely gave on the cross, He gave us salvation for our souls if we seek Him and the grace of the Father. We now have the right to reach out to the Father in prayer and seek forgiveness of sins through repentance. When we repent all our sins to the Father and ask for forgiveness, the just Father and faithful God will forgive our sins. There is no sin too great that the Father will not forgive as you come humbly to Him. He is a loving, caring, and grace-filled Father waiting patiently for us to come to Him for salvation. Never think that your sins are too great to be forgiven. With God, all things are possible. His will is that He doesn't want anyone to perish and be thrown into the lake of fire, which is for the devil and his demons. All you have to do is come to the Lord, seek forgiveness, turn away from sin, and live in the spirit of the Lord Jesus Christ.

Serving the Lord

It is You, Lord, that I seek
With a broken empty heart
It is You only
Who can put this broken heart back
To the point of living again
It is You, Lord, I want to serve
For all time
In Your Holy Spirit
Let Your will be done on earth
As it is in heaven
It is You, Lord
Who makes my light shine
In the darkest of night
Fill me up, Lord
With Your Holy Spirit
Until I am overflowing
You are a lamp unto my steps
And a guide unto my heart
It is You, Lord,
I long to serve forever and ever!

Kingdom and Dominion

We are all well aware of the rise and fall of various kingdoms that existed for centuries, ruled by men and women who held dominion over all the kingdom's subjects. Not all rulers who exercised their authority were fair, just, and kind. We know of many rulers who besieged their citizens, mistreated them, exploited them, and killed them for no reason but for greed and power. Many ruled as sovereign authorities, oppressing citizens under their leadership. Is this not going on in today's world?

When God the Father created the universe, He created all things that we witness today. At the time of creating mankind, God placed dominion over all species of life under humankind's authority. God was pleased with His work. Peace and joy and freedom reigned supreme until the sin of Adam and Eve. That brought into the world sickness, pestilence, disease, sorrow, pain, and death. The Father became disappointed and angry over the temptation of man by Satan, who had no regard for the kingdom of God on earth. Satan wanted exclusive dominion over all creation.

The devil, we know, is a murderer who steals, kills, and destroys, not caring who he harms as long as he can declare himself ruler of all. We must stand bold in the power of the Almighty, relying on the Holy Spirit. It is our duty to let Satan know his dominion over us is false, and we will not fall into any of his traps.

God's kingdom is not of this world but brings everlasting *life* to all those who believe and trust in Him. Jesus did not conquer death to allow Satan to fill you full of his lies. Jesus did that to prove that Satan has no power over Him and that you have the same power in His (Jesus's) name. God wants your life in Christ to have such an impact on the lives of others that they come to the Father and repent, never to rely on the flesh again. God has given the keys of His kingdom to the Body of Christ, the Church, which the gates of hell cannot prevail against. We are the body of Christ, the church of the living God, and we have been sent into this world not just to witness, but we are sent to take it back and put Satan under the Father's rule.

The Father says that whatever we as disciples ask, He will give us.

> Ask of Me, and I will give you the nations for your inheritance, and the ends of the earth for your possession. (Psalm 2:8)

May we always cherish and respect the kingdom of God and realize that He has supreme authority and dominion over all.

About the Author

I turned my life over to the Lord at a young age. I asked Him to come into my life. But I didn't want to give in to what it took to live a happy life free of worries, heartache, and misery. Once I made Jesus my Lord and Savior, my life is much happier and more filled.

Printed in the USA
CPSIA information can be obtained
at www.ICGtesting.com
LVHW091541221024
794497LV00002B/332